# Walking with Wallace

Michael Koe

# Contents

# Introduction

THE AUTHOR, MICHAEL KOE, WOULD like to point out that neither the views expressed by him in this book, nor those attributed to his Grandson, Archie, on their walks with his dog, Wallace, are necessarily actually their own. Whose, then, are they, you may wonder. Well, the point the Author is primarily looking to make is in relation to his comments (and Archie's) on quantum physics and related subjects. These comments, which hopefully you will read and inwardly digest as you progress through these chapters, are largely extracted from and based around the Author's understanding of various books on quantum physics that he has read. The Author acknowledges that he may have misinterpreted some of these and doesn't want anyone thinking, potentially mistakenly, that what he has written is necessarily gospel.

Wallace, too, might well wish to point out that some of the views he is quoted as expressing are not his, either! *'Walking with Wallace'* is, therefore, correctly designated as not primarily a book designed to educate the reader on quantum physics nor is the Author actually quoting his dog! Wallace's given views are, however, as close to Michael's perception of his thinking as possible, as too are the scientific and philosophical facts he debates with Wallace and his grandson Archie, (of whom you will hopefully read more later), on their walks together. This story is essentially a real life account of their walks in the beautiful South Northamptonshire countryside, during which Wallace, Archie, when around, and the Author debate important philosophical and scientific issues of concern to man and dog. .So, too, is the relationship between Michael, his family, his Grandson Archie, Wallace's predecessor, a fine Staffordshire Bull Terrier (Staffie) named Wilson and, of course, Wallace himself.

Wilson, Wallace's predecessor had been 'rescued' from Battersea Dogs' Home by Michael's son Jamie and proved to be the most gentlemanly and well behaved Staffie possible, despite his attraction to and skill with the rugby ball. Due to the pressure of Jamie's work and life in London, Wilson's visits to Michael and his Wife, Sara in South Northamptonshire increased to the point that he, Wilson, was relocated to live up there and became Mummy's Staffie, on a more permanent basis, with an implicit transfer of ownership, though his allegiance to Jamie remained strong throughout his short life. Wilson deserves his place on these pages for the honour and loyalty he showed in his short life, as the pathfinder Staffie, preparing the Author for Wallace's later arrival.

Wallace, easily identifiable from the photograph on the cover, was a handsome and loving Staffie. He and the Author lived under the same roof (and at night, it must be admitted, after some skilful early maneuvering by Wallace, on the same bed), over thirteen years, during which time they probably saw more of each other than of any other living creature.

The Author, whose lovely wife, Sara, sadly died from a devastating neurodegenerative disease in 1995, has, in his eyes anyway, four brilliant sons, four beautiful and brilliant daughters in laws and thirteen wonderful grandchildren, all of whom he and Wallace saw as often as possible.

You, like them, the Author hopes, might like to read more about Wallace and him, (known to his Grandchildren and referred to throughout this book, as 'The Brig') and their walks and philosophical debates.

Finally, the Author would like to thank all those who have so generously helped him, in different ways; a special thanks to both to Debbie Benadie, for her hours of proof reading of content and to his family for their patient encouragement and helpful input in putting this book together.

# Chapter I

## *In the Beginning*

THE BRIG, WAS - AND still is - a keen amateur cosmologist. He avidly reads newspaper articles about the latest discoveries in particle physics, quantum mechanics and black holes. He keeps on his desk a list of questions about the universe, life on other planets and on dark energy, dark matters and other important related philosophical issues. He would often discuss these with Wallace (and Archie, when around), during their walks through the beautiful countryside in which he lived.

*Wallace ponders matters in the garden*

Despite Wallace's tendency to be distracted by what was going on around him and to keep his thoughts to himself, he always appeared to have as good an understanding as any on these issues. Anyway, The Brig felt he knew him well enough to be able, when in doubt, broadly to interpret his thoughts, though he accepted not always correctly, for Wallace could, at times, be remarkably unpredictable.

On a clear, sunny, spring morning, as The Brig turned the key in the garden door, Wallace, as usual, magically materialized alongside him. They crossed the house's paved terrace together, climbed up the two steps on to the still wet lawn, sparkling in the early morning sunshine and made their way on up the gentle slope of grass to the top gate. This opens onto a small extension of the next door Church's cemetery, with a public footpath running left and right to the green fields beyond. As they moved left through the cemetery, Wallace was, unsurprisingly, up ahead, full of energy at the start of his morning walk.

Passing through the cemetery extension, their interest turned to the rows of ageing tombstones. As Wallace meaningfully approached one, The Brig felt himself travelling back through time. In his mind's eye, he dwelled on the comparatively short lives of those buried there. He looked back on his own life and the happy years with his late wife, Sara, and their four sons, as they grew up.

He pictured Wilson, his son Jamie's puppy, romping in the grass in the garden of the house, where Sara and he had lived, when they had 'inherited' him as their first Staffie. He recalled stories about these wonderfully loyal, brave and handsome bull terriers, brutalized in the eighteenth century and trained to fight to the death in cellars in the Staffordshire mining country. His thoughts went on back to their breeding from bulldogs and terriers to their powerful and aggressive ancestors, used in battles in Roman times.

He thought too about his own, at that time, powerful and aggressive Viking ancestors (he recalled his Father telling him and about his Danish Great-great Grandfather, who apparently had sailed over peacefully enough from an Island near Copenhagen, to set up as a barrister in Scotland and then moved to Ireland, around the time that Darwin was born.

Charles Robert Darwin, as he reminded Wallace, was the scientist, whose book *'On the Origin of Species'* spelled out, to a disbelieving World, his theory on this, that was to challenge accepted view on this controversial subject across the World. Their thoughts about Darwin and evolution quickly transported The Brig, in his mind's eye, back to the emergence of the human race from the animal and fish world, then further on back to the beginning of life itself on earth and then on back to the formation of the stars and galaxies and on and on still further, to some 13.5 billion years ago, to the Big Bang itself, the very creation of the Universe.

"In the beginning—I mean in the very beginning, not when you nor I came into this world, nor even when our ancestors arrived", The Brig remarked to Wallace, as the latter sniffed the grass close by a nearby tombstone. 'Neither you nor I, nor any living creature was around in any recognizable form, though each of us, I suppose, could have been a part of a huge cluster of unspecified quarks (elementary particles and fundamental constituents of matter). Everything that is anything in our Universe started with the 'Big Bang'. This was the moment of creation, when time and space began and our now majestic universe grew in a few micro-seconds from near nothing into an unbelievably hot, ever expanding fiery ball of fundamental particles that make up all its and our constituent parts'.' Wallace nodded sagely, as though all was becoming clearer.

In less than a minute, The Brig continued, our universe had grown to over a billion miles across and was still expanding unbelievably fast, doubling its size every second. "Everything you can now see, feel or touch just grew from this miniscule black hole, far smaller than the size of a full stop."

Wallace looked annoyingly unimpressed, toying at some earth next to a gravestone, no doubt thinking 'what was the Old Man on about' and why should we bother about when and how the Universe started or worry about its size some 13.5 billion years ago. No one he knew was around then and no one he knew really cared how it all began. He certainly didn't. Probably, in his view, there was quite enough going on in the here and now on this beautiful morning to keep everyone happy, without such irrelevant distractions as fundamental particles.

Admiring his philosophic acumen, but sensing his lack of historical perspective, The Brig ploughed on -it had to be said, without engendering much further interest in what was rapidly becoming a rather one sided philosophical monologue. He half apologetically added, to anyone still listening, that such scientific assertions had always fascinated and worried him. "Perhaps", he suggested to Wallace, "The Universe around us was formed from the immensely compressed contents of the death throes of another dying universe or even from nothing, surrounded by nothing; though, if just nothing, one had to ask what, if anything, did this nothing consist of? And what was going on before that Big Bang? And what was around that black hole, when it arrived; more of this nothing?"

Some astronomers, he recalled, reasoned that, put another way, nothing consisted of equally balanced quantities of plus and minus 'half nothings' or, in more scientific terms, of exactly balancing of matter and anti-matter particles. Whenever a particle of matter meets a particle of anti-matter, the pair will, they tell us, like true warriors, annihilate each other- back to nothing (with the tell-tale emission of gamma rays). In which case, The Brig wondered why all the matter around us had not been annihilated by its anti-matter pair? And, since it had not, where had all that missing anti-matter gone? "Is it even now hanging around, waiting its moment, and if so where, he asked, as Wallace moved off toward a nearby tombstone.

'Was he too wondering where those antimatter particles had gone; or even whether they were hiding there behind that nearby tombstone, for that certainly had his full attention', thought The Brig. More likely, he feared, just sniffing out another mark.

It was, he reflected, anyway, an extremely difficult question even for our brightest scientists to answer satisfactorily, particularly in light of recent experiments at CERN (The European Centre for Particle Physics) in Geneva. The Large Hadron Collider there accelerates, to speeds near that of light, particles travelling in opposite directions through its 34 mile long elliptical tunnel under France and Switzerland to a designated narrow section, where such particles either narrowly miss or collide with each other. These near speed of light collisions, which mimic conditions in the universe a few trillionth of a second after the Big Bang, have successfully (without blowing the world apart as some had forecast or feared) created, albeit briefly, small quantities of antimatter, confirming its existence.

At the time of the Big Bang, anti-matter was, cosmologists assure us, around in large quantities. Its disappearance and the existence of dark energy and dark matter, they believe, all play crucial roles in the balance, and even existence of our expanding Universe. Their experiments, too, support the strong theoretical and mathematical evidence that ordinary (positive) matter represents only 4% of the universe, with dark matter representing some 23% and dark energy the rest, a massive 73%. "You've lost me", thought Wallace. "Stay with me", said The Brig, it will all become clearer over time."

"Let's just get this walk done", thought Wallace. "Stop rambling and start marching". "We must talk more about this dark matter and dark energy later", said The Brig, who anyway was already finding it extremely difficult to get his own head around some of these cosmological propositions. He also feared Wallace was no longer paying the necessary attention and that he would currently be wasting his time in asking him his views on such matters or, indeed, on anything else.

However, the possibility that, before the Big Bang, there was no time, no space, no anything but the eternal present stretching back for ever, chimed well with Wallace's focus on the 'here and now', thought The Brig. Wallace's expressive brown eyes made it clear too that he was much more interested in the eternal present than the distant past, though he was prepared to reflect briefly on the more recent past (possibly breakfast) and the near term future (probably lunch), before returning to the present and continuing to size up the next nearby tombstone.

The Brig hastily pulled him away, thinking though perhaps he was right. Shouldn't we all just be enjoying today; for it goes so quickly and it is that which we do here and now, over which we have at least some control? Wallace would certainly have argued that that was what was of over-riding and immediate importance. However, as any historian worth his salt would have done, The Brig reminded him, that what happened in the past has always been an instructive and invaluable guide for our decision making today, which will, in turn, affect our future.

The start of the universe still clearly has great relevance to what and where we are today. Without its creation and miraculous development, neither he nor Wallace, he pointed out, would be enjoying the sunshine or their walk. In fact, neither they nor anyone else would have been enjoying anything at all here on earth as neither the earth nor the stars would have existed. Giving him an intent look, Wallace ignored this riposte and pulled on his lead. The walk must go on.

It was some thirteen years earlier on the human clock or just over ninety one on Wallace's, that he, the main character of this book (as by now you will have guessed!), and his two sisters arrived on earth. The Brig had first met Wallace in a house in Birmingham where the latter had lived for the previous six weeks of his then extremely short existence. Wallace, or 'Kara's Red Flame', as his official kennel name importantly and improbably described him, was lying contentedly on his back, between his rather smaller sisters, with his chubby legs pointing languidly in the air. He gave the impression of being aware that he was the pride of the litter.

*Puppy Wallace examines The Brig's shoe*

The Brig had meanwhile been observing him closely as a prospective companion. He was a well set, broad shouldered, straight legged Staffordshire Bull-Terrier, with widely spaced eyes, a strong jaw line and apparently without fear. Under closer inspection, he just calmly rolled over, once again, onto his back, waiting for his tummy to be rubbed. Then with a grunt of pleasure, when this service was given, he shook himself, got to his feet and pressed his broad right shoulder against the visitor's leg.

Selection had not been difficult, for The Brig had been immediately captivated by this dominant, alert bundle of loose flesh, mischief and inquisitiveness, with large, expressive, intent, fierce and, when necessary, melting brown eyes, a black muzzle, a white patch on a deep chest, a long and powerful body, one white sock and a long whippy brown tail.

His paws were enormous, with more white patches underneath. His ears, or oysters as they are sometimes called, were soft and silky to the touch and unbelievably expressive. He was, in short, a strong soft Staffordshire Bull-Terrier puppy, full of all sorts of wickedness. Rolling over, he pushed his clearly adoring sisters aside to investigate more closely this potential owner. With one intent look, he decided that this Visitor might just do; and that was that, for The Brig was hooked and quickly agreed with the breeder's steep terms and a collection date.

After a short get-to-know-you session, he had then left, pleased and excited to have found 'Kara's Red Flame', whom he instantly re-named as 'Wallace'. It had to start with a 'W', like Wilson, his predecessor and anyway The Brig couldn't see himself, with his voice echoing across the South Northamptonshire countryside, calling out 'Kara's Red Flame', every time he wanted him to 'come to heel' (though he soon learnt, this was not a term that Wallace lightly recognized).

So he returned to Wappenham, to prepare for Wallace's arrival, with purchases included a large 'living room' cage, assorted bedding, hair brushes, feeding bowls food, leads and other puppy impedimenta. Fortunately there was a thriving veterinary practice in nearby Towcester, who could handle all the necessary injections and vaccinations, sold many of the requisite products and provided some of the technical advice required to keep Wallace trim and healthy - well healthy anyway!

Two weeks later, Wallace came home, in a large wire cage, in the back of the Brig's car, very miserable and rather car sick on the journey. The latter was some £500 the poorer, but far, far richer in quality of life and companionship, with his new acquisition. On arriving back home, he cleaned him up and made a big fuss of him. Wallace wagged his tail furiously and, quite tired after all the excitement of his move and journey, curled up in his well-padded cage for his first night at Wappenham and was soon gently snoring.

Before Wallace's arrival those years ago, The Brig had lived alone for some three years, since the dark days of his wife, Sara's illness and death—well, not really alone, for even before Wallace had arrived, there were plenty of other members of his close family popping in and out of his life.

The Brig had been brought up close to the Wiltshire Dorset border, and after schooling in those counties, he joined the Army, and saw service around the World, including postings to the then 'West' Germany, Hong Kong, Cyprus and Washington DC, as an Exchange Intelligence Officer, at the time of the personal confrontation between John Kennedy, then President of the USA and Khrushchev, then President of the USSR.

This confrontation took the World to the brink of nuclear war between these two superpowers. For, at that time, Soviet trawlers, with the necessary equipment to complete the installation of nuclear weapons in Cuba, were approaching that Island. Kennedy then informed Khrushchev on a telephone hotline, open to the public, that he would order the sinking of these trawlers, unless they were stopped immediately and withdrawn.

The Americans had, at that time, several squadrons of bombers in the air, armed with nuclear weapons, ready to fly to and destroy Moscow, if so ordered. To the immense relief of all, Khrushchev, faced with this clear threat, backed down, as the World stood on the edge of nuclear devastation.

The Brig had also served in West Germany Hong Kong, Penang, Borneo, Cyprus, Northern Ireland and for three tours over six years, Berlin. One of those three was with the British Mission to the Soviet Commander-in-Chief's Forces in East Germany, involving 'touring' in fast cars ('souped up' Opel Admirals and Range Rovers) from the Mission House in Potsdam, through the beautiful wooded villages of East Germany; followed closely by their Soviet counterparts, each side taking great interest in the other's disposition and movements. It was an exciting and remarkable cold war experience. The Brig had retired, after two years in Rheindahlen in West Germany as Brigadier General Staff Intelligence (BGS Int), (hence 'The Brig') in the late seventies.

Further back in time, he had married the lovely Sara (then a 'dizzy Deb') in the late fifties. Before her devastating death in 1995, they had had some thirty six years wonderful years together They had travelled the World, had four great sons, now with four beautiful ''daughters-in-laws' and thirteen exceptional (of course!) grandchildren, whom, particularly after her death, he visited as often as he could, or, perhaps more accurately, as often as his long suffering daughters-in-law would have him and his dog to stay—for this normally now meant not just him, but Wallace too!

Despite these visits and his many friends around, The Brig (having retired), at this stage of his life, saw each day, more of Wallace, than of any other living creature; and their walks were the highlights of their daily lives together and, of course, an important opportunity for philosophical debate.

Their favorite route took them through a kissing gate into a large field, across which the footpath meandered past the next door farm, over a stile or, if villagers preferred—and most did—through a gap in the hedge alongside it, into a second forty acre field. The footpath across this ran down to a small lake some quarter of a mile wide, some half mile in length and well populated by wildlife on the surface and by fish below, with a right of way causeway along the North Side to the far bank. The lake itself was attractively edged by trees, bushes and fields. It had a well-organized and popular fishing community and, on sunny days, many of this community could be encountered with their rods, casting for trout and other species in the lake.

On this particular day, as The Brig and Wallace left the Cemetery extension and farm behind them, they continued on through the gap in the hedge, down to the lake. Up above them, the sunshine and bright blue skies concealed from sight the trillions of stars up there, many of which can be observed with the naked eye on a clear starlit night.

Looking up to where they were hidden by the brightness of the sun, The Brig mentioned to Wallace a scientific article he had just read about the search for planets inhabited by living creatures across the Universe. For, amongst all these trillions of stars in their billions of galaxies, cosmologists now accept that there are millions of other planets across the Universe at the right distance from a star, that, given water, would be capable of sustaining life, some perhaps inhabited by weird and wonderful living creatures and more than a few possibly with greater intelligence than ours.

"A recent study" he informed Wallace, "indicates that some small percent of the hundred million stars in the Milky Way alone, are likely to have planets in the 'Goldilocks' zone, neither too hot nor too cold for water and hence life to exist. There is even a possibility" he asserted (in what was, with the number of stars in the Universe, a near infinity of possibilities), "of some world out there, with canine like creatures having humans as their pets".

Wallace looked happy about that, but perhaps wondered, in that case, about feeding arrangements. Some humans might have to get by on wholemeal biscuits, he thought with a small inward chuckle. "If only we could talk to some of these living creatures out there, even just across the span of the Milky Way", The Brig then added, "We could then be sure, rather than statistically confident, that they exist, and learn something about their lifestyles".

Wallace looked thoughtful about that. However, as The Brig then pointed out, there were some serious technical difficulties in communicating with alien life (even more than those that sometimes occurred when he sought to communicate with him). These difficulties were not just those of language and understanding, but of time, since nothing[1] can travel faster than light and light itself takes thousands of years just to get from one side of our own galaxy to the other and a lot longer from other galaxies.

So a major practical problem in intergalactic communication with other living creatures, with sufficient skills and intelligence to communicate at all and understand each other, is the number of light years that separate us from them. This could make conversation of any sort infinitely time consuming and difficult - different reason perhaps but a similar outcome to when Wallace and he sought to debate a topic of mutual concern.

Of course, time warps and wormholes might, as described in some science fiction, enable messages or even creatures from distant galaxies to arrive much more quickly. However, these alternate methods and routes, he understood, could be extremely dangerous to take, if they existed at all and - a bit like conversations with Wallace - were probably just confined to fiction.

The Brig reminded him of an article he had read about the launch of NASA's Kepler Probe and its recent successes. This probe has already found some planets in our own galaxy, not so far away, that are at least capable of supporting life (not too near and not too far from a friendly star—the 'Goldilocks' zone). Early findings from its mission include that of a sun-like star amongst the some 160,000 in its current field of view.

Despite this star being some hundreds of light years from earth, Kepler still has been able to identify that it has five earth-like planets, one of which appears to meet the 'Goldilocks' criteria—neither too near or too far from their sun. Kepler 22B, for example, is a planet eerily like the earth with a temperature of 22C and a sun of similar

---

[1] *A fairly recent experiment appeared to contradict Einstein's long accepted theory that nothing could travel faster than light. In this experiment, neutrino particles were timed travelling between CERN in the suburbs of Geneva to the Gran Sasso laboratory near Rome—a distance of some 730 kilometers. A system of detectors showed them to have completed their journey around sixty billionth of a second faster than light. However, these surprising results were later found to be caused by a fault in the buried fibre-optic cabling or oscillator and new readings taken in a repeat experiment in May 2012 confirmed Einstein's conclusion.*

size and distance away to that of ours. If it holds water, it is likely to hold life.

But even for a similar star, with life supporting planets within our galaxy considerably nearer than that, it would still take quite a few years travelling close to or at the speed of light for any message we sent to reach its inhabitants and a similar delay before the alien could reply—other than through the aforementioned wormholes.

"That however, might turn out to be no bad thing", he suggested to Wallace. "We really don't have any idea of the sort of creatures (that might live on these life supporting planets), who we are seeking to meet and know; and their tendency might be, if they have the intelligence and technological skills, either to kill or colonize us, utilizing our potential in a similar manner to that we apply to animals here on earth."

Wallace recognized that that would certainly be bad news for humans, who might have to put up with some of the constraints that domesticated canine species have to put up with on our planet. The Brig sensed his reasoning and a related thought occurred to him. "If ever, Wallace, we could surmount the technical difficulties of reading the minds or at least understanding the language of other creatures here on earth, forgetting, for the moment, those on other planets across our galaxy, we might listen more and perhaps, as a result, adopt more equitable arrangements when dealing with them".

Wallace was well prepared to point out his thoughts on this. For, to him, it was obvious that from the viewpoint of an impartial visitor to Planet Earth, human-animal relationships, in broad terms, would today fall under one of the six categories he outlined in his mind (set out below), in which animals are utilized to provide the human race with one or more of the following-

    i.   **Transport and Sport**—horses ,donkeys, camels, elephants etc

   ii.   **Medical Research Material**—monkeys, mice and other animals for trialing potential drugs, without risk to human life.

iii.   **Game**—to be photographed, shot, hunted down or fished.
iv.   **Livestock**—to be eaten as and when required.
v.   <u>**General Support Animals**</u>—to retrieve, 'protect', or carry.
vi.   **Pets**—and, of course, pets to be petted

Taking this last category, few animals, apart from dogs (and, to an extent, Wallace grudgingly admitted, cats) made particularly good pets. Many other species were possibly equally attractive or interesting to some humans, although a fair proportion needed to be kept confined in cages to protect their owners and/or their owners' neighbors or even the animals themselves.

Even for pets that can freely roam around the house, The Brig felt that it was often a rather one sided relationship, with the pet being encouraged and trained to fit in with their family's lifestyle. Cats largely opt for independence and accordingly just slip in and out of their owners' lives. Dogs are much more interdependent, Wallace reflected, and often spend the great bulk of their day lying down, waiting for their 'Master' or 'Mistress'—as they so arrogantly call themselves—to take them for a walk or give them a pat on the back or some biscuits.

The Brig reminded Wallace that most behavioral psychiatrists would argue that dogs were bred out of wolves and establishing yourself as 'The pack leader' was the key to successful human canine relationships. Teaching your dog early on to obey commands, such as 'stay', 'sit', 'wait there', 'down boy' etc. are, they suggest, essential to ensure a harmonious lifestyle living together.

This is good advice, certainly from a human perspective, but you might suspect that dogs would consider the deal to be rather one sided. Wallace, he knew, certainly would and, in some ways, so would he. In their complex relationship, he did not particularly want all the time to be *top-dog* or 'boss', with a hard to envisage, highly disciplined Wallace leaping to his command.

Like many other dog lovers, The Brig was deeply aware that those they single out to become their 'pets', often become much more than that. In return, they receive single hearted and unconditional love and companionship, which other humans often fail to match.

Wallace, he recognized too, had quietly and gently found a small corner of his heart, moving in there to join other members of his fast growing family.

# Chapter 2

## *Young Wallace*

***Young Wallace with a punctured ball***

AFTER THE FIRST HOMESICK FEW days, clearly missing the warmth, love and attention of his two sisters, Wallace began to settle into and enjoy his new life with The Brig. Each night, to begin with, he would sleep in a wire cage in The Brig's bedroom. Although he whined a little at first in his new home, after a while it became a safe base for his further adventures.

His daily routine at Wappenham started around 7am with the opening of the cage, and an exploration of his new surroundings.

Wallace loved exploring The Brig's house and would often be seen inquisitively sniffing around doors and peering into new rooms. If he met a human on his travels, he would invariably bound up to them, offering immediate friendship and the occasional lick.

As soon as he remembered, The Brig would take Wallace outside into the garden, so he could 'do his business'. Wallace would quickly respond to The Brig's requests that he 'be a good boy', finding a suitable bush to crouch behind, modestly even for a young and guileless pup. This exercise was followed by the daily (initially quite short) walk. For Wallace, this was a tremendous affair. The chance to widen his surroundings and to explore new territories. There were so many sights to see. No need to consider the nature of the universe at this point, better to just enjoy it!

After a quick lap of the garden and the local fields, young Wallace and The Brig would return to the house for a rewarding breakfast. Wallace would devour some Farley's Rusks laid on by The Brig, perhaps with some hot milk for seconds, while The Brig would have some coffee and try and read the paper; often, with little success as young Wallace would then jump up on his tummy looking for a place to rest. Once The Brig roused himself to go to his office, Wallace would follow and commence a mid-morning nap on The Brig's helpfully positioned sofa.

Around eleven o'clock, there would be a biscuit for the young pup and playtime, during which Wallace would chew an old sock or slipper, throwing it up in the air and catching it, hoping someone would join in and try and take it from him. He was very quick but surprisingly gentle in this game.

During this play time, Wallace would growl and bark with pleasure as he leapt around with a tremendous surge of energy, before going back to sleep until lunch time. For lunch, he had slightly less than half a tin of puppy Pedigree Chum, which he ate voraciously, if there was nothing better around. However, even at that age, human rather than dog food was clearly his preference.

As far as 'proper' food went, he was a good trencherman, though not particularly greedy. He quickly made it clear that he was not that keen on dog biscuits, particularly once he had tasted red meat from the butcher. The Brig would admit later that he may have given Wallace a taste for this delicacy perhaps a little too early, but would never think it a mistake. It made Wallace very happy and life after all should be fun and full of treats, should it not? Wallace, however, did become a bit of a picky eater, and would sometimes, as a puppy, just walk away and leave his meal; only returning when driven by hunger to the humiliating acceptance of being fobbed off with a tin of Pedigree Chum.

All his life, Wallace regarded every human as his friend, unless it became very clear to him that this wasn't the case. He would rush up to every new companion (and those he already knew) and show his friendship and loyalty, often by offering licks and other physical signs of friendship.. Although sometimes slightly confused and saddened when humans were not so keen to accept his 'jumping up' friendship, it didn't put him off one bit.

Wallace also assumed that his unconditional love of the human race, both individually and collectively, would always be reciprocated in all circumstances. It never occurred to him that his size, and Staffordshire Bull Terriers' reputation, might make some fearful of him. He adored children and put up with any treatment by them, giving, in return, surprisingly careful and gentle love.

As Wallace grew and matured, the cage soon became too small for him and (with The Brig's at first reluctant acceptance) he soon moved at night upstairs and onto the bed, settling down close to the feet of the old soldier. The 'next morning' routine would then invariably begin (often, after a night punctuated, judging by some of his endearingly excited squeaks, by dreams of the chase) with some stretching and rolling, before a visit up the bed and an offer of a surreptitious lick to ensure The Brig was sufficiently awake to start the day.

Once The Brig had been entreated, cajoled, licked and bullied into actually getting out of bed, washing shaving, dressing and completing his boring morning exercises, during which routine Wallace would lie at full stretch on the carpet, with his head resignedly between his paws and his legs spread-eagled behind him or alternatively rolling on his back with legs in the air, whilst waiting for the eagerly anticipated collar-putting-on-routine, they would then set off from the bedroom downstairs together.

As they both aged, Wallace tended to spend more of this time curled up on the bed, waiting his move until he heard the key in the garden door –hopefully, walk time, at last! Early morning walks, at all times other than the occasional day in the winter months, became the highlights of his young life. The mounting excitement of keys in the door and emerging into the morning sunshine could be seen reflected in his eyes and energy levels. And on their walks, they were almost never further than an extending lead's distance apart. As they crossed the nearby fields in the beautiful South Northamptonshire countryside, The Brig would begin to debate with him the great philosophical issues of our day, such as the Universe, the meaning of life and other deep moral concerns affecting man and dog.

Wallace would enter the debate, either with a knowing look or gesture. Sometimes, though, he would just listen and grunt in agreement and sometimes just eye the Brig intently. As a puppy, he rarely paid full attention and contributed no more than a swish of his expressive tail, though his intent look indicated that he clearly understood, even though he did not necessarily agree with what was being said.

The Brig continued to assume, perhaps wrongly, that he knew, or could figure out, from Wallace's expression, his views in their debates. Wallace was, however, growing into a remarkably perceptive and intelligent dog and often by his actions, challenged this assumption. He had strong views on most things—even (or perhaps mostly) the immediate direction of their walk—though the former still retained some control over the overall route. There was a wide choice. However, many involved a short drive from the house to the start of the nearby walk.

On car journeys, Wallace liked either to sit in the front passenger seat, or, if this place was occupied by another passenger, to lie at full length, facing the rear between the driver and front passenger seat with his hind legs stretched out, straddling the stubby gear stick with front paws firmly on the back seat—outwardly an extraordinarily uncomfortable balancing act! Reluctantly, at The Brig's insistence (who explained to Wallace the consequences not only to him, but to anyone in the firing line, of thirty kilos of dog flying through the windscreen, should the car stop suddenly), he accepted the need to be belted up, that is clipped in, with a safety harness..

He would settle in his harness, between the front and back seats of the car. On arrival at the start of their planned walk, The Brig would park the car and, once the putting-the-lead-on exercise was completed, lock it. Then off they would set together. It was, as usual, a field or two before a philosophical issue was debated and many fields further before they returned to the car, physically and mentally exhausted , certainly as far as the former was concerned,

On their return, Wallace, temporally well exercised, would lie under or even occasionally on the desk in the Brig's office or, as he grew more independent, sit on the window seat next door, perhaps thinking about their latest philosophical discussion, but more likely sleeping or, in the latter location, viewing anyone passing by; and keeping an eye out for that ugly black cat, who lived nearby.

The Brig, whenever he was away for a day or two and unable to take Wallace with him, would ask one of a carefully drawn up list of 'dog sitters' living in the area, to come and look after Wallace and the house—in that order! For, apart from the issue of leaving the house empty and unguarded, he remembered when Wallace had had his first two day trial at a nearby kennels, which had frankly not been a great success!

Wallace had first sought to fight a large black Labrador and, when put in a cage, wouldn't eat any of the dog food he was given. During the day, he just lay curled up in an unhappy ball. That night, he started mournfully howling. The owners, who lived next to the kennels, clearly did not enjoy the night chorus, as, one by one, the other inhabitants joined in.

Despite this unhappy start, he would probably, with discipline and time, have learnt to accept that kennels were part of a dog's life. However, just before The Brig was going away next time, and this time for a full week, a young family, who lived in the neighborhood, offered to take Wallace to their home, a nearby farm, during the former's absence. They had a puppy of their own, and the two got on famously, not only with each other but with two fat ginger cats on the farm. An outdoor entertainment for all four was stalking cows in a nearby field.

Wallace was, one memorable day, also taken to a rugby match in Northampton, which he enjoyed immensely. Early on, he had sought to join in the match itself, and show, like his distinguished predecessor, Wilson, his skills with a rugby .ball. Fortunately for all concerned, he was on a short lead and firmly checked, preventing him from doing so. The family, on The Brig's return, indicated that it had been a great pleasure to look after him and that he had been much admired by their friends! From then on, Wallace looked forward to his visits there, whenever The Brig was abroad. And for shorter absences, local 'house and dog' sitters were booked in.

South Northamptonshire is blessed with much beautiful open countryside and large wooded areas, so there was a wide choice from which the Brig could select from, for their daily walk, though quite quickly the lake route had become Wallace's favourite. This was probably due to the attractive young golden retriever who lived nearby and wandered freely between her home, the farm at the top of the hill, and the lake.

As the Brig and Wallace left the cemetery and abutting field, they spotted her lying like a pale shadow in the dark green grass by the causeway, where the footpath widened into a track to cross the earth dam at the foot of the lake. Seeing them, she leaped up to greet Wallace, overjoyed and wriggling with pleasure, before rushing around him in tight dizzy making circles.

She had been spayed, so was neither particularly interested in Wallace's rather un-gentlemanly direct approach, nor his excited marking, but very happy to join him and the Brig on their walk up the hill past her farm, where her owner, as usual, would come out to recapture her yet again. She had built up quite a reputation around the village of being wickedly naughty and would regularly lead Wallace and other hopeful male dogs a 'merry dance' between the lake and the farm.

As Wallace marked the grass nearby, the Brig admired the spectacularly beautiful scene in the early morning sunshine, with the still waters of the lake mirroring the green, brown and yellow of the lakeside trees and grass. Canadian geese, ducks, dabchicks and moorhens paddled slowly around, with the waters quietly rippling in their wake. The smells too were intoxicating, even for a human. Wallace, like most canine species, owned some fifty times the number of scent receptors of the average human, so the scents that day for him must have been overwhelming. The Brig observed him suck in, like a vacuum cleaner, the odour in the grass; his legs braced and attention absolute.

At that moment, it was apparent that nothing else in the whole wide world mattered to him. This was the present. The past and the future were irrelevant. Concentration was absolute. What information was there for him to glean? Clearly, a great deal, from the time he spent sniffing around and assessing the exact spot to mark his visit. On completion of this important task, his attention was drawn to a small movement at the far end of the lake. The Brig had long admired Wallace's remarkable eyesight and ability to spot any movement at a phenomenal distance. His thoughts turned to this miraculous process, which enable us to see at all; and to be able to observe amongst other objects, the beautiful things around us. "What is this beauty and how do we actually see it?"

"And why do we think what we see is beautiful?", he asked Wallace, who looked up quizzically in response, although clearly more interested in the scent and the young golden retriever than what he made clear, by his look, was, in his opinion, a pretty stupid question. However, he immediately acknowledged by his actions that beauty is indeed in the eye of the beholder, for it was obvious that he found the golden retriever extremely attractive.

Undeterred by Wallace's rebuff, the Brig continued. "Photons in their billions, as they are formed from intensely hot bubbles of gas in the sun, move off in every direction at the speed of light. Those hitting the earth bounce off their target and some, (those coming your way) in turn, strike the retina of your eye, where they are absorbed to form a picture of that object the eye is focused on. This involves the photon being turned into energy". "This level of energy", the Brig reminded Wallace, "can be calculated, using Einstein's famous formula, e=mc squared, where 'e' is the energy, 'm' the mass and 'c' the speed of light. Thus, the energy derived equals the mass of the photon (which fortunately is far, far smaller than an atom), times the square of the speed of light (186,000 miles per second)."

"The brain then uses this energy generated in the retina of the eye, to form a picture, before rotating it through 180 degrees, so in our mind, we see the right way up. The neurons in your brain routinely carry out this almost miraculous function to enable you to see", The Brig pointed out to Wallace, adding "like many other actions they perform, you and I take these amazing capabilities we are given entirely for granted, unless or until something goes wrong". Wallace hoped the mass of a photon was indeed very small, otherwise it occurred to him this might be a painful process, with these mini atomic bombs regularly going off in his eyes.

The Brig added, "For example, over there, you can see a pair of beautiful Canadian geese" pointing across the lake. Wallace had spotted them in the rushes several minutes ago and had been keeping a sharp eye on them ever since. He sighed. The old man was off again! Still in his philosophical mood, The Brig continued, "To me they appear beautiful, but what is beauty and why is it beautiful? And when seen, in whatever form, why does such a sight lift one's spirit and add joy to the day? Is it a gift from the universe's designer or some evolutionary process of our mind's eye, perhaps performed by our evolving genes? In other words, is it an anthropomorphic biological trick, as Darwin would have us believe, or a gift from God?" Wallace gave him another withering look and turned away.

The Brig, undeterred, continued, "Looking at the exquisite design of a simple daffodil or even a blade of grass, I find it hard to accept that what we see has all, over time, just been made possible by super- heated sub atomic particles". It was harder still, he felt, not to see a designer's hand in all this and other such near miraculous processes, even taking account of natural selection remaining at the heart of successful evolution.

Wallace heaved yet another sigh. He was clearly not willing, at this time anyway, to be drawn further into this sort of, what he considered to be, pointless debate. As they moved up the hill, he was, anyway, still intent on admiring—now at a distance—the beautiful golden retriever, who was by then well ahead of them, approaching her home, where her owners were calling. She was, as usual, duly recaptured and marched firmly inside.

After the Brig and Wallace had left the area of the farm house and the re-captured golden retriever, Wallace made a few half-hearted attempts to turn back, but, after being dragged by his lead a metre or two, initially reluctantly, but with increasing enthusiasm, moved forward down the track, sucking in, with renewed zeal, the scents around.

Reverting to his earlier thoughts on improving human/animal communications, the Brig wanted to hear more of Wallace's views on sight and beauty; and, of course, on the aforementioned philosophical issues, like the beginning of the universe, the creation and the purpose of life. Would Wallace argue, he wondered, that a dog, like a human, had a conscience and a soul (and if not, at what point in evolution would he reckon these were conferred on the latter?).

Not wishing, however, to travel too far down this potentially controversial route, the Brig decided to return to his theme of celestial time and the start of life on Planet Earth. Wallace was, by then, fully absorbed by the enticing smells from the deep grass and flowering shrubs on either side of the farm track that led to Bucknell Woods. "Here we go again", he thought, as the Brig regained his attention with a sharp pull on his lead.

"Wallace", he said "we should be clear on how life of any sort was initially formed on earth. You know, of course, that the earth was spun off from the gases that made our sun (and solidified into a sphere under subsequent gravitational pressures) some 5 billion years ago and that, since then, different sized meteorites have, over the last two and a half billion years, occasionally struck our planet?"

"Of course", muttered Wallace to himself. The Brig added "Did you know, too, about the enormous heat caused by fusing protons and electrons into simple elements like hydrogen and helium?" Wallace nodded affirmatively—anything to keep the old man happy!

"However", the Brig continued, "thanks to Professor Brian Cox and his television series broadcast on Sunday evenings, nearly everyone now knows that the heat at the centre of a star the size of the sun is insufficient to enable the necessary level of nuclear fusion or nuclear synthesis to take place and thereby 'build' the more complex elements. These, however, are essential for the chemical action that produces the amino acids needed for the construction of live and living creatures. Without them, life on earth, of any sort, would not exist. "So, how did these more complex elements, higher on the Periodic Table, come to exist on earth?" Wallace was clearly unable, or unwilling to answer this crucial question—crucial to life, that is.

The Brig's grandson Archie, had he been present at that time, would inevitably by now have asked, "What are Elements and what is the Periodic Table, Grandpa?" The Brig explained to Wallace that the simplest element, hydrogen consisted of a single atom with just one proton and one electron circling around it.

"Nuclear synthesis", he continued, "can bind atoms together to form more complex elements, with additional protons (with a positive charge) and electrons (with a negative charge)—and to complicate matters, neutrons (with no charge). The electrons circle around the nucleus of the protons and neutrons. The more complex the element, the higher it sits on what is called 'The Periodic Table'.

This Table lists all the 108 elements that exist across the Universe, in the order of the number of protons and electrons they contain. Those higher on this list have neutrons as well as protons and electrons. Those near the top of the list are considerably less stable. Such complex elements, however, can only be produced/ manufactured through the death of much larger stars than the Sun— at least ten times its size, like, for example, Betelgeuse. They are called Supernovae. Their deaths are rare and, fortunately for our planet, have so far, been distant events", The Brig added, for good measure, "Since if they died nearer than some ten light years away from the earth, we too would all be burned up".

Wallace looked perhaps a little concerned about that 'so far' qualification. The Brig continued "In the incredible heat (the equivalent of many thousands of nuclear bombs simultaneously exploding) as these Supernovae burn out at the end of their lives. They first expand dramatically and then, as their supply of hydrogen diminishes, shrink into incredibly dense balls, known as black holes. So dense, in fact, that even light cannot escape their gravitational pull. In this process, simpler elements like hydrogen and helium in the unbelievably hot furnace at their core, combine to form these more complex elements".

Wallace looked up expectantly, either showing greater interest in what he was hearing, or perhaps more probably hoping for a mid-morning biscuit. Ignoring the latter interpretation, the Brig continued "This takes us back to these meteorites. Once they started arriving, with their complement of elements higher on the Periodic Table, the consequent chemical reactions on our primordial Planet Earth led inexorably to the creation of life forms".

The Brig could visualize such primitive life forms emerging in the dank, dark, hot caves on Earth. He pictured, where there was water, the amazing variety of life forms slowly evolving, including strange fishlike creatures emerging from the sea some hundreds of million years ago, leading, over time, to the astonishing range on earth today—of which only a small fraction (some two million species) have yet been named. These 'Life Forms' evolved to produce creatures like Dinosaurs and later, Neanderthals, Homo Erectus and, near the end of the line. to date, Homo Sapiens.

"So, Wallace," the Brig added, "if and when we trace back our ancestors far enough, we have to conclude that both yours and mine probably came as fish from the sea. Going back in time, but not so far, you would be able to trace your lineage from the canine species, of which the Bull Terrier breed is part, back to wolves, from which dogs evolved." Wallace was not surprised by this but clearly flabbergasted at the thought that one of his early ancestors might have been a fish, as would many of us.

The Brig reminded him that competitive genetic evolution had led to an astonishing range of life form, including, for a brief moment in time, both him and Wallace. How would their descendants –if any - evolve over the next million years? As they approached Bucknell Wood, he would have liked to have had time to discuss this, to him, fascinating evolutionary quest further, but that would have to be on another day, as it was, by then time to return home. Furthermore, as they continued down the grassy overgrown track toward this wood, Wallace clearly had other things on his mind, and was no longer giving the necessary attention for such a debate to continue.

The Brig, looking at his watch, reflected how quickly time passed when you were enjoying life, each day seemingly ever more quickly. Hardly had he drawn the curtains in the winter months in the morning, he felt, than he was closing them again at night, with Wallace, nearby, observing his actions with interest. Perhaps life would end in some future winter with time passing so quickly that he would permanently be standing there opening and drawing curtains. If so, he would hope to continue to see Wallace's inquisitive look as he did so.

He reminded himself that time was, anyway philosophically speaking, 'relative'. Life of any sort has only been around on our planet for a mere fraction of celestial time. The universe itself was still quite young, with an estimated nine trillion years or so of life left before the billions of stars up there burnt out to reach the closing stages of their lives; to, what some cosmologists argued, that moment a few trillion years ahead, when the cold emptiness of space would only contain shrinking black holes, dark energy and dark matter; and, in the end, the lights in the sky would go out, as our Universe just reverted back to nothing.

The Brig recalled those biblical words 'from nothing we came, to nothing we will return'. However, more encouragingly, other cosmologists argue that new stars are constantly being born in the space created, as the Universe expands. He also recognized that the sun was not yet half way through its allotted time, with some five million years' worth of hydrogen left still to burn, so there was no immediate concern. Indeed, looking back, life on earth had only existed to date, in any recognizable form, for about that time. The odds, too, against the human or canine species existing on earth at all today were, at the start, very long. The probability of Wallace and him being around, even taking account of Darwin's theories on evolution, must have been approaching infinity at the time of the 'Big Bang'! Of course, in a universe full of infinities anything was and is possible, though it seems unlikely that the human race will still be around on earth to worry about that in five million years' time, when the sun finally burns out.

Time, however, as Einstein had demonstrated so conclusively, varies with speed. The faster you move, the slower it moves. At the speed of light, time just stops altogether. Everything then remains in the present, in line with Wallace's thinking and preference. However, as his maximum speed was about half that of the garden squirrel, a hundred and eighty thousand miles per second was somewhat above his ceiling.

Recent data from an American observatory hunting for warps in time, not only offers evidence of the first minute of the universe's and perhaps time and space's existence, but of the resultant gravitational waves of the 'Big Bang' itself and their effect on time (that the observatory's laser beams sought to measure). "Scientists at the observatory", he assured Wallace, "can now predict, with confidence, the maximum wavelength of these space-time ripples, (which originated with the 'Big Bang') and expect to be able to measure the actual change of time, as they pass through their laser measuring devices. All of this work – though difficult for most, including the Author, to understand - supports Einstein's conclusions that without space there is no time; and that time is relative to speed."

Wallace's view was that time was much more relative to waiting for the next meal or the next walk, than to ripples and warps in space, whatever they were, but recognized that it was anyway relative to species. For, what is one hour, on the human scale, is some seven for dogs or, using a similar measurement scale, some two years in the life of a fly, assuming each lives to the equivalent of 100 human years. On this basis—forget the fly—both Wallace and The Brig had at that point reached over three quarters of what was expected to be their respective species average life span.

For, today, only a few currently living humans on our planet have, themselves, been around for more than 100 years and few dogs live to fifteen. This was, the Brig reflected, an unpalatable fact—sad too from the viewpoint of how long Wallace had left, making their remaining time together all the more precious and their walks more memorable, even without their debatable philosophical content.

Scientists forecast that, for future generations of humans anyway (if they don't, in the meantime, wipe themselves out one way or another), their allotted time on earth is likely to increase noticeably—some suggest that for babies born in 2050, a hundred and fifty year life span will not be unusual. The Brig's youngest Grandson, Walter, and his older cousin Archie were both accordingly likely to live well into the twenty second century, unless some unforeseen event like climate warming or some devastating virus wiped them all out. Unhappily, he reflected, our 'canine companions' lifespan is much shorter than humans and all dog lovers have to face the probability of a day when their pet dies or has to be put down, (a mealy mouthed euphemism, he felt) unless they themselves die first, in which case their pet's future is often very uncertain.

He reminded Wallace that his presence on earth was due to the long odds chance of his distinguished forebears meeting and of his mother giving birth to a litter, in which he was, incidentally, the sole male. The Brig also reminded him that he kept in a desk drawer in his office Wallace's official Kennel Club papers and certificate of pedigree, which confirmed that he had been born on 27th April 1998 and certified, (clearly correctly) as a male Staffordshire Bull Terrier. He was then, as mentioned earlier, named at birth 'Kara's Red Flame', presumably because he had short reddy brown coat (as opposed to brindle or black and white) and because his Mother had a second name 'Kara'.

His Sire had been 'Walbert Nut Cracker', his Dam' official name 'Tanygrisiau Girl' and his Grandfather (a Cruft's Champion!), as aforementioned, was 'The Red Brigadier'. His Grandmother had been named 'Amazing Grace'. With the Brig's military rank and his late wife Sara's reputation, both he and Wallace shared these two rather unlikely links in common.

Wallace had been briefed on the history of Staffordshire Bull Terriers. He knew that he could claim Bulldogs, Mastiffs and Terriers amongst his more recent ancestors. The former two, large, ferocious war-dogs, were taken by the ancient Britons into battle against the Romans and proved to be both courageous and terrifying combatants.

The crossing of these two larger dogs with the more agile smaller Terrier breed some 800 years later (to form the Bull-and-Terrier or Bull Terrier) took place at a time when dog fighting had become a fashionable sport. The breeding of these smaller, faster dogs, full of courage and fire, then led to a wide variety of Bull Terriers.

The Staffordshire Bull Terriers came, Wallace knew, from a Black Country background, where some were trained to fight each other (with large sums of money being put on the outcome by the crowds who watched this 'sport') in Staffordshire cellars.

They were still, as a result, sometimes confused with the truly ferocious American Pit Bull Terrier, bred solely for fighting. It was not, however, until 1935 that the Staffordshire Bull-Terrier was accepted by the Kennel Club as a pure bred variety. Their loyalty, intelligence, courage, handsome looks and love of family are today widely admired and recognized.

However, they are immensely strong and powerful for their size; and with inherited fighting genes, those deliberately trained to be aggressive and the 'bad eggs'- as 'bad 'eggs' do even exist amongst the human race—inevitably, though rather unfairly, have somewhat tarnished their reputation in some quarters, as those families who own these wonderful and loving dogs quickly learn.

Wallace was not, in fact, the Brig's family's first Staffie. Wilson, like Wallace, was a 'Staffie' too, but very different in character, size, pedigree and background. Although they never met on this earth, Wallace, as mentioned earlier, shared many genes with Wilson and, despite their different characteristics, they had much in common. Both were much loved by their family, both were remarkably intelligent and loyal, and both were powerful and handsome Staffies.

# Chapter 3

## *Enter Wilson*

UNLIKE WALLACE, PEDIGREED TO HIS aristocratic toenails, Wilson, although also a pure Staffordshire Bull-Terrier, came from a deprived and unhappy background. Aged some six months, he had joined the Brig's family, in what could only be described as the most improbable of circumstances.

The Brig's son, Jamie, had been taken to Battersea Dogs Home one summer by a then girlfriend called Nicky, who, at that time, rented rooms in the basement of Jamie's and his elder brother Simon's house in Shepherd's Bush. Jamie had intended to do no more than just accompany her and view, at a safe distance, the assorted canine species there, but had spotted young Wilson, looking oddly vulnerable, curled up by his cage, dejected, unkempt and very much alone.

As a handsome three month old puppy, he had been found abandoned, half-starved and tied to a post in Battersea Common; and, from there, taken to the Home. When Jamie saw him, he was unsurprisingly nervous, cowering away as if to ward off a blow from anyone who approached him. Nicky, after one look, unkindly summed him up as an undernourished urchin, though she did confess, in a motherly way, that he looked rather sweet. Wilson took an immediate fancy to Jamie and stumbled determinedly after him as he was leaving the room, with an appealing and desperate gesture for help.

Jamie always pretended to be tough, but underneath was generous and soft hearted, and hated to see any animal in distress.

Although he had not had any intention of acquiring a puppy that day, he melted under Wilson's intent gaze, and, having completed the necessary paperwork to confirm his naming and ownership of Wilson, took his new friend to his car. Wilson was a hugely grateful, overexcited, deliriously happy puppy who was would do anything for his new Master. The Brig assumed that Jamie had named him after Harold Wilson, though Jamie told him later, that it was an altogether different connection. The Brig decided to ask no questions.

Nonetheless, for the Brig and his wife, Sara, he was always Harold Wilson. Wallace had heard, over the years, much about him. He was regularly reminded by The Brig of Wilson's upright character and life, his absolute obedience, his gentleness, his gentlemanly demeanor and immaculate behavior both in London and in Northamptonshire. Wallace was distinctly unimpressed by this information. Although they shared many genes, he clearly had reservations about any relation of his whose behavior was that good. He naturally assumed too that, with the passing years, the Brig's failing memory had added gloss to some of the stories of Wilson's uprightness and meekness. He certainly couldn't believe that any Staffie worthy of that name and breed had never been involved in a fight. For the Brig had told him over the years, the full story of Wilson's life from when he had been taken from Battersea Dogs home and settled in with Jamie at Shepherd's Bush.

Jamie, who had just started his own business, had, at that time, taken him with him each weekday morning to his offices in central London. In the spring, summer and autumn, Jamie would bicycle through the London traffic, with a long hand-held rope lead at the end of which Wilson would gamely run, dodging the cars, buses and taxis coming the other way. Each day, he became a braver, faster (well, the traffic on central London roads was, even those years ago pretty heavy) and, with Jamie, happier puppy.

In the colder winter months, they went more securely on foot and by underground to Jamie's offices, where Wilson happily soaked up affection and biscuits from the staff working there. After an idle morning, he would then enjoy a lunch time walk in the nearby park and look forward to the often incident- packed journey home in the evening.

Gradually his fear of humans subsided. Over the next couple of years, Wilson grew, both in size and confidence, into a handsome and loving Staffie, though his underlying nervousness never entirely disappeared. If Jamie raised his voice against him, Wilson would lower his whole body and creep cowering to his bed, flattening himself as if to ward off the next blow. Routine mistreatment in early life had clearly left its mark.

Wilson himself was never aggressive, nor ever growled—and he never even looked like wanting to fight another dog. In fact he was, in character, the perfect gentleman, careful, attentive and unassuming. And loving. The Brig had to remind Wallace, on many occasions, usually after a misdemeanor, what a great example Wilson had been of how a Staffie should behave.

Such reminders did not go down well with Wallace. What a pathetic 'goody goody', he thought to himself. Wilson had adored Jamie and been entirely happy just to be with him. On their visits up to Northamptonshire, the Brig and his wife, Sara, had soon learnt that he was a very easy dog to look after. He had few, if any, vices except for the tendency to stray off and make new friends with anyone around and a strange habit, given the chance, of dribbling rugby balls, at which he was remarkably skilled.

Jamie took him for regular evening walks through Ravenscourt Park in London (usually not on a lead). Occasionally, he would disappear, having been lured away by a particularly attractive scent or otherwise distracted, usually reappearing after a few minutes with a broad smile and a metronomic tail wag. It was, however, not unusual for Jamie to have to track him down and find him in a nearby pub or betting shop, where he had been 'taken' by new friends' having just 'strung along', after yet again, a friendly word from a stranger.

With Jamie working increasingly long hours, as his business grew, he found it ever more difficult to have Wilson with him all day and give him the relationship, the love and the walks he craved. Sometimes, Jamie's older brother, Simon, or young Nicky, would be at home to look after him, but very often he had to be left for longish periods alone in his basket. Then he would lie there curled up, miserably awaiting either the 'dog walkers' arrival or Jamie's return home.

Always ecstatic and never reproachful, he would wriggle all over with joy as one of them opened the door to greet him, but it was obvious that he did not enjoy those long hours of basket time on his own, nor those long evenings when he was left in the car, whilst Jamie was out at dinner.

Wallace recalled the hours he too had had to spend in the car, whilst the Brig shopped or dined in the warmth of a friend's house nearby. As Jamie's workload increased, Wilson's visits up to Northamptonshire gradually built up from weekends to longer stays. He loved the open country and walks down to the canal; and he loved Sara - who made a big fuss over him - almost as much as he loved Jamie.

Back in London, he disappeared yet again one summer evening on a walk in the Park. After nearly three unsuccessful and increasingly desperate hours search, Jamie reported his loss to the police, who warned him that Staffies were very popular as guard dogs and status symbols in that part of London and that it was, they feared, highly likely that he had been stolen with that in mind. Distraught, Jamie put up posters with a picture of Wilson and a notice in all the nearby shops, along the lines 'Lost, stolen or strayed, one handsome red Staffordshire Bull Terrier, called Wilson. Generous reward offered for his safe return'.

Two weeks went by, after which Jamie began to fear that this time he had gone for good. However, a 'third party' then telephoned and said she had seen Jamie's ad, and that some friends of hers had a dog just like Wilson. She said they had found this young Staffie wandering on his own around Ravenscourt Park and taken him in. She gave Jamie their address but said that by now they felt they owned him and obviously would not be happy parting with him— she hinted that money might have to change hands for his safe return.

Jamie set off immediately and found, at the given address, a group of young men in a rather unsavory, dilapidated and over-crowded flat. In reply to his initial enquiry, they all shook their heads, but when a reward was mentioned, one of them admitted that he had taken home a young Staffie he had 'found' in a park, wandering around with no owner, a few weeks earlier. He now considered himself to be the owner. Jamie then offered a small reward and no police involvement in return for an immediate return of his dog.

After some haggling, a door was opened and Wilson rushed out. He looked half starved, but alive and well and overjoyed to see his master, with his tail going like a windmill and wriggling all over. Jamie afterwards confessed to having had to pay what looked like quite a substantial ransom, but was so relieved and happy to have him back, that he was content with the outcome. He decided not to take the issues of 'theft' or blackmail to the police.

Wilson's visits up North, after this incident, soon extended to the point where The Brig and Sara felt they were gently being offered Wilson's ownership! Not that they minded, as he was an immensely loyal, loving, friend, undemanding and easy to look after. Jamie, of course, denied that was his intent. However, as his business grew, he recognized that keeping Wilson in his house in London was putting quite a strain on both of them; and reluctantly agreed the compromise of sharing him as a family dog. He recognized too that Wilson had become very attached to Sara, as 'Mummy's Staffie'.

*Sara with Wilson 1994 (Photo)*

The Brig and Sara had, at that time, bought, badly in need of love, attention and money, a rather run down Elizabethan Manor House built in 1540. It boasted a Great Hall, a Minstrel's Gallery and 'Solar' (a room from which the ladies could look, from an internal window, down into the Great Hall, where they could observe their husbands carousing), on the edge of a village near Northampton.

Their lifetime aim had become to restore it to its former glory. When Wilson joined them there, he found the countryside and wide choice of walks much to his liking; and soon settled in with their two Persian cats— rather simply named 'White Job' and 'Blue Job'. Blue Job had achieved fame in their family, having accidentally slipped on the sill of a top floor window, some thirty foot above the gravel drive below, then somehow 'floated' down with limbs and tail akimbo, free fall parachutist style, landing with a tremendous thump but without any apparent damage, other than to her pride. Sara, then in the kitchen, had watched dumbstruck Blue Job's descent and was amazed to find her intact on the gravel, shaking herself as she regained her footing but with no visible ill effect from her fall.

With age and a loving family, Wilson had, by now, lost his terror of the past. He was always overjoyed when Jamie came up for visits and weekends, which he did whenever he possibly could, so the change of home base was not too challenging, though he still clearly missed his 'Dad' and the rush of London life.

Throughout his life, he displayed an amazingly peaceful nature and unlike most Staffies, never once did he ever snarl or even look aggressively towards another dog, even when severely provoked. Wallace regrettably occasionally failed to inherit this trait and, particularly in his youth, displayed his impressive fighting qualities, fortunately without damage other than to the pride of his opponent of the moment, on three memorable occasions described later. Wilson quickly and happily settled down in his new home in the beautiful South Northamptonshire countryside, with long walks in fields, on and off the lead; and with Jamie coming up for weekend visits—giving Wilson the best of both worlds.

**Wilson on the prowl at Gayton Manor**

Whenever he was offered the opportunity, he continued to develop his rugby skills, particularly with The Brig's sons, chasing or dribbling the ball, with his dexterous nose, A few months after he moved up north, The Brig took him one afternoon to watch one of his younger sons playing in a school rugby match nearby. Wilson suddenly and entirely unexpectedly decided to join in and, to the embarrassment of The Brig and astonishment of the spectators, mostly anxious parents, took off from the touchline, trailing his lead (in hindsight, insufficiently firmly held) and dribbled the ball from one end of the field to the other before returning proudly to his family, with a big grin and wind milling tail.

Fortunately, although like Wallace in later years, he loved chasing and dribbling a rugby ball, unlike Wallace, when he had 'captured' it, he did not then set about 'killing' it (this would sometimes be the result of Wallace's footballing technique, to the discomfort of The Brig, who would then feel the need at least to offer to buy its owner a replacement ball).

On this occasion, as the ball was taken, undamaged, from the home side's twenty five to their visiting opponents try line, astonished Mothers and Fathers and other home team spectators were not sure whether to cheer or glower at Wilson's Guardian at Gayton. However, both of them were thereafter watched closely, particularly by the opposing sides' parents.

The Brig and Wilson often met other dogs being walked along the nearby canal, including, on one day, another young Staffie. As the two groups approached each other, The Brig asked its owner anxiously whether it was a 'boy' or 'girl'; for Wilson, though not a fighter, was not keen on other male Staffies. She said it was a 'girl'. After a brief conversation, The Brig asked her what hers was called. To his astonishment, she said 'Margaret Thatcher'. He then introduced her to 'Harold Wilson'. She laughed. The two dogs meanwhile formed an instant attachment. Although they met again several times along the canal, their brief courtship—regrettably—never developed to the point that might have led to a Thatcher-Wilson dynasty.

For, a few weeks later, Sara hit her head hard on a sharp edge of scaffolding, whilst pushing a barrow load of rubble near the outbuilding and knocked herself out, inflicting a nasty cut just above her right eye. Wilson, who was there at the time, was clearly upset by this, and was reluctant to leave her side for the rest of the day. At the nearby surgery that afternoon, the doctor put in a couple of stitches above her eye and everyone expected her to recover quickly, but it didn't work out that way. Gradually and imperceptibly, a series of little concerns, like a slight unsteadiness, dislike of bright lights and tunnel vision, all hard to put your finger on, began to emerge and worry her and her family.

Sara had been a stunningly attractive debutante in the late fifties (they still existed then and had much fun, as such) and had, at that time, been a very part time Secretary at the Post Graduate School of Medicine in Harley Street, living nearby in her Grandparents' apartment. She had become interested in and knowledgeable about medicine and always kept a small library of obscure reference books, through which she now pored, seeking to match her difficult to define symptoms.

For, in addition to worries over her eyes and emerging problems with vertical gaze (she couldn't look up at the ceiling or down at the floor, without moving her head), she had had a growing fear of falling backwards, sore eyes, a stiff neck and, a new symptom, tiny cramped handwriting. Meanwhile, her GP appeared to be at a loss as to the cause. The ophthalmologist to whom Sara was referred could not detect anything basically wrong with her eyes.

Then, worryingly, a CT scan revealed what was described as some shrinkage in her brain, which is associated with alcohol problems, but Sara did no drink. It was several month s later, after several frightening and unexpected falls backwards, that she was finally referred to the National Hospital for Neurology, where she was diagnosed by a doctor—later an eminent professor there— as having a comparatively rare, slow moving but ultimately fatal neurodegenerative disease, first described by Steele, Richardson and Olszewski, three Canadian Neurologists, in the early 1960's. It had become known as 'Progressive Supranuclear Palsy', now more widely recognized by its initials, 'PSP'.

In early 1994, The Brig and his family were forced, as the symptoms of this grim disease progressed and Sara became wheelchair bound, to move from their lovely early Elizabethan Manor House, (which was, by then, sadly quite unsuitable for Sara, with its sweeping stairs, different levels and stone steps), to an Old Rectory, next to St Mary's Church in Wappenham, an attractive small South Northamptonshire village some ten miles away.

Things meanwhile steadily worsened for Sara. As time went by, she found it harder to swallow. Her balance was going and soon speech became more difficult. Her vision, particularly up and down gaze, was failing. She was also finding it hard to read and watch television. Attractive, intelligent, energetic and outgoing, only in her early fifties and full of vitality and life, it was devastating for her family to watch helplessly this deterioration in her health and capability over the next two years. What it was like for her, was difficult to imagine. She showed, however, immense courage and grace throughout these remaining years of her life.

Their new house had a large fenced-in garden with a door in the hedge and fence some hundred yards up the hill at the far end, leading through a small extension of the Church Yard Cemetery to endless fields and wonderful walks, though Wilson was by now reluctant to leave Sara's side. As wheelchair outings became more difficult with winter approaching, he spent more and more time, lying on the floor, legs stretched out behind him, close to her. He remained her most constant and faithful companion, during her illness, so bravely borne.

On 20th January 1995, Sara was admitted to Northampton General Hospital with 'aspirational pneumonia', a not unusual complication of late stage PSP. The Brig understood that, with treatment, she was likely to recover from this quite quickly and be discharged in good time for their son Richard's graduation with first class honours in history from Oxford the following Monday.

He accordingly left her around seven pm that evening to return home to meet up with Jamie, who was driving up from Wiltshire to see her the next morning and then attend the graduation ceremony. Just after midnight, they were called from the hospital. Sara had died a few minutes earlier. They then drove from Wappenham to Northampton on a cold, clear starlit night to make a last visit to a now seemingly empty small room in the General Hospital, where for The Brig, the reality that Sara and he had spent her last day on earth together slowly sunk in. Amid the grief and pain of her loss, there was relief that she was no longer facing the misery of a daily decline in the quality of her life, which had already, with the loss of the ability to communicate with the outside world, reached the point where she struggled each day to face the next as the quality of her life steadily worsened.

They had been married for 36 years. After dreary administrative and funeral arrangements which followed, there were the long winter days when life to The Brig seemed pretty pointless, though, at that time, as he told Wallace later, he genuinely felt her presence and her faith (She was a staunch and strong Catholic) to keep him going. His four sons were brilliant and set up a very acceptable duty roster of visits to entertain and help look after the 'old man' and Wilson up at Wappenham.

Wilson too was devastated by her loss—for weeks after her death, he would rush to the door when someone arrived to see if it could possibly be her. He clearly missed her dreadfully, but kept The Brig company through the dark hours of the night. Each day, they went out together for walks across the beautiful Northamptonshire countryside. Wilson loved it at Wappenham and was a great companion to The Brig, now living on his own. By 1996, however, aged nine, the former too was noticeably slowing down. Grey hairs had spread from his chin to his muzzle and he had quietly but gradually over that year become an old, but much loved 'gentleman'. Climbing the stairs had become a bit of a struggle and he moved in the morning much more stiffly. He still loved lying on his back in the grass outside the house in the sunshine, rolling backward and forward and still greeted any new arrivals at the house with wriggles of joy, but curling up by the fire in his basket was becoming more the norm.

When he became reluctant to finish his meal and unenthusiastic about going for a walk, or even a stroll, in the garden, it became apparent that this was not just ageing; he was not well. The Brig accordingly took him to the vet in Towcester, who felt he should come in for a more thorough investigation. She feared he had developed testicular cancer, which might have spread to his liver. She recommended an exploratory operation to find out how far the cancer had spread, for, it was becoming clear that he had, for some time, been uncomplainingly putting up with much pain.

The Brig was shocked, however, when she then asked him for his agreement to put Wilson down, if she felt effective treatment was not possible. After some discussion, he then reluctantly agreed for her to do what she felt necessary, if she judged it to be best for Wilson. She telephoned him that evening, on his return from London, to confirm that the cancer has spread throughout Wilson's poor body and she had, as agreed, given him a lethal injection, following which he had quickly, painlessly and peacefully died. The Brig remembered with anguish the last look and lick Wilson had given him earlier that day. Dog owners will know well the heartbreak of this final act of mercy.

For those like The Brig, who regard their dog as part of their family, the final stages of their time together on earth can be quite stressful. With the marked difference in human and canine expectations of life, there comes, however, the almost inevitable moment that all dog lovers dread—the 'decision time', as their pet nears the end of his or her pain free life.

Putting a dog down is usually done in what is genuinely believed to be its best interest—to prevent him or her suffering unnecessary pain and misery, when the quality of its life is judged to be falling and already below an acceptable level. The Brig had heard that some brave owners just shoot their dog in the end to give it a quick and comparatively pain free death. Most, however, lack that sort of courage and take it to the vet for a lethal injection. That last journey can be agonizing.

"So why do we feel it perfectly OK", The Brig asked Wallace lying straight legged next to him, "to have the dog we love put down, when we feel he or she is 'ready to go' (where?), but we can't or won't (in this country anyway) help those humans we love who can't help themselves, in a similar way, when they face what can be the last painful and miserable stages of their existence on this earth? Is it that we have a soul and dogs don't?

Or does our conscience tell us that it is wrong to help someone to die? Or perhaps it is more a question of a legal deterrent to discourage old and infirm people from feeling they should do the decent thing and make way for the next generation, but need some help in doing so; and/or to deter the latter from being tempted to 'help' rich and unwanted relatives on their way?

If the law in the UK were to be changed, would this be a slippery slope, as the population grows and ages, or would it give those who wish to die the right to do so, helped if necessary? This whole subject was very topical in the UK at that time, but when The Brig raised it with Wallace, he appeared increasingly disinterested, looking at The Brig inquisitively, with a half-hearted wag of his swishy tail. This sort of philosophy was not his strong point. He was probably thinking

"What does it matter what I think? It won't make any difference to what they decide and do, when the time comes".

The Brig reflected morosely that Wallace had a point on that bleak decision. Wilson's worldly remains or ashes were by then in a small box on a shelf in the Old Rectory. His DNA (Deoxyribonucleic acid) can be found there. This DNA contains the entire coding for his construction. Pointing this out to Wallace, as they continued on their walk, The Brig reminded him about Darwin and Mendel's evolutionary theories; and more particularly about Wilson's immortal genes.

He had had no offspring to pass these on to, though many identical genes to those he carried are carried today by his living relatives. Wallace felt that that knowledge would probably be of small consolation for Wilson—hardly the same thing as living again himself. Nonetheless, it was time to explain to a reluctant Wallace a bit more about genes.

The Brig liked to think he listened patiently, even though patently not as intently as he would have hoped. "Inside that box there are cells", he began, plagiarizing from newspaper articles and drawing on his involvement in a medical charity, "containing DNA and protein, making up genomes, which provided for him, as for all living beings, the genetic coding or information needed by their living cells to specify (as expressed by their genes) their structure, function, activities and interaction with other cells and the environment".

"Oh yes", thought Wallace, concealing a yawn, wondering perhaps whether the next generation of Staffies would have a gene ration like his. The Brig went on "The DNA itself forms a double helix made up of two strands of sugar phosphate 'axons' twisted around each other, bonded by what are called base pairs, each consisting of two of the four nucleotides, (Adenine (A), Thymine (T), Guanine (G) and Cystosine (C). 'A' only bonds with 'T' and 'G' with 'C'."

Wallace looked tiredly away. The alphabet had never been his strongpoint. To rouse his curiosity, The Brig suggested that he should picture himself climbing a twisted ladder, whose rungs each had a letter on either side, where they joined the uprights. So a rung might consist of an 'A' and a 'T' or vice versa, or a 'G' and a 'C' or vice versa.

"Imagine", he suggested, "climbing, like the Ribosome 'reader' (a complex structure made up of more than fifty different proteins, which reads off these letters and follows the amino acid recipes embedded in the DNA coding; then uses the coding to build the species as instructed), up one side of the ladder and down the other". Wallace hated heights and the thought of climbing up and down a twisted ladder made him quite dizzy. The Brig added that the ladder would have to be a pretty long one, as the human genome contains, within its genes, some billions of these four letters to be sequenced. The precise sequence of the four letters read off (three letters at a time) along the full length of the two sides of the 'ladder' then provides the code, or gene expression, which enables the Ribosome to instruct and bind together the required proteins (the building blocks of life); and, accordingly, as this code changes the form of life itself changes too.

The Brig was, by now, in full stride, "Mathematically", he continued, "there are four to the power of three or sixty four possible combinations of letters in each of these resulting sequences. As there are only twenty amino acids required and involved (making the neurons, muscles and fibroblasts needed to construct the species) in constructing a life, there are more than sufficient combinations to provide the necessary codes to control this process. With sixty four choices and twenty different acids, some of the instructions are just to 'start' or 'stop' the process and some are as to how much of each amino acid is required. The process is strictly regulated and controlled in the transcription and translation of these sequences into a living being".

By this stage, Wallace was looking more than a little dazed. "What is the old man driveling on about now—the thought of all those rungs and instructions makes my head spin", he muttered to himself. He thought too that although most humans he had met were generally pretty smart and in some areas possibly even more intelligent than a Staffie like him, it was a pity that God had not given them better vision, hearing, sense of smell and, more relevantly to the current debate, greater common sense. They might then take more interest in things that were really important, like walks and meals and less in endless stuff like the building blocks of life. Wallace sighed, as his talkative owner rabbited on, discussing with himself things that Wallace was pretty sure he didn't fully understand.

Theoretical concepts and abstract ideas had never been his specialized subject, not his preferred discourse. He was not sure that he would recognize a gene if he saw one, anyway! At that moment, his attention was sharply distracted by a particularly attractive scent and he moved off to investigate. By now, The Brig and Wallace had left the lake far behind, after a steep climb and then a long hike up a muddy footpath, which continues up the hill toward Bucknell Woods, where, there is a car park at the main entrance to these 'open to the public' woods, with various tracks and footpaths leading through the two to three square miles of forestry commission land.

There are usually, particularly in the summer, other dogs and horses being exercised and plenty of wild life to be sniffed and squirrels to be chased. The occasional roebuck added to the excitement of Wallace's walks there. The biggest problem with Bucknell Wood walks was, however, that, except in midsummer, anywhere off the limited main tracks, the footpaths quickly became, particularly in the winter and after rain, waterlogged with swamps, streams, felled trees and broken off branches, making progress really hard going.

It was easy to slip and Wallace and The Brig had often stumbled back to the car, covered respectively nose to tail and head to foot with wet, clinging mud. That was OK for an old car, but not so good after The Brig had purchased a new one. These woods, nonetheless, were high on Wallace's walk list, though a fair distance from home; and time was getting on. Reluctantly, particularly as it was such a beautiful day, The Brig decided to give up on their increasingly one sided debate on genes and the construction of life and order an 'about turn'. He was pretty sure Wallace hadn't been listening as attentively as he's hoped.

Wallace, after a sharp tug on his lead, reluctantly complied with his owner's request. So they retraced their route back past the farm and Wallace's girlfriend, then on down to the causeway and from there up the hill back home. The Brig meanwhile agreed, given a sunny day, to drive to the car park at Bucknell Woods for a proper walk the following week, when his eleven year old grandson, Archie, would be staying and would be keen to accompany them. Archie loved Wallace; and really enjoyed walks and scientific discussions. Wallace loved Archie and enjoyed walks. The Brig loved them both and enjoyed both walks and scientific debate. They all loved Bucknell Woods. All three would therefore be well accommodated.

# Chapter 4

## *Enter Archie*

**Archie and Wallace set off together**

BUCKNELL WOODS ARE ABOUT A mile east of Abthorpe, a village that lies between Wappenham and Towcester. The following Sunday, The Brig's grandson, Archie sat comfortably in the front seat of the former's new Volvo—with Wallace lying less comfortably with his tail and bottom between the driver and front seat passenger and his head on the back seat, the extraordinary position he regularly adopted when deprived of his favourite spot (upright on the front seat). The Brig drove carefully, with his precious crew, along the road from Wappenham to Towcester, turning right at the crossroads just after Abthorpe onto a country lane, which leads to Silverstone, passing by, en route, Bucknell Woodland its Car Park, a mile down the lane on the right.

On arrival there, the three 'debussed', leaving the car with the many others in the car park, and set off up the main footpath into the woods, with Wallace forging ahead excitedly on his extending and extended lead. When other walkers approached, The Brig enquired politely, at a safe distance, as to the sex of their dog. If the answer was 'male' or if there was no reply, the oncoming dog would be given a wide berth. If female, Wallace was allowed a brief introduction, with tail going like clockwork—assuming the oncoming owner was willing to say hello, which they usually were. This, in turn, often resulted in entanglement of leads and much tail wagging and excited breathing, until The Brig pulled the protesting Wallace away.

As they reached the less populated part of Bucknell Woods, a Mobjack (the woods were well populated by these small deer) hurtled across the path in front of them. Wallace sought to give chase, but The Brig sharply checked him on his lead. Archie, too, was very excited and enquired about deer in the woods. He asked, in particular, if any reindeer lived there. The Brig thought it unlikely but, under pressure, agreed that it was possible. As he then explained to Archie and to Wallace neither of whom showed as much interest as he would have liked or the subject deserved—that anything is possible in our Universe as Heisenberg, of Quantum Mechanics fame, had first hypothesized in his 'Principle of Uncertainty'. This Principle, which is now widely accepted by scientists, confirms the obvious-if-you-think-about-it conclusion that given an infinite number of choices, anything is possible. In a clever and mathematical way, he demonstrates how particles (which can move simultaneously, as a wave, in every way possible, from one point to another) escape from black holes, confounding the laws of gravity.

Archie, of course, asked what a black hole was. The Brig reminded him that the level of gravity on the sun's surface today - due to its mass - was about twenty times that of our planet—so any space ship passing too close would be subject to sufficient gravitational pull to be sucked in, crushed and torn apart before being incinerated. Wallace looked concerned about that.

"A black hole", The Brig continued, "is the remains of an even larger star that had exhausted its supply of hydrogen". At this stage of its 'life history', the star, if large enough, would after a brief explosive expansion, then contract rapidly in size (but accordingly increase in density and hence mass and gravity). Its gravity at some point becomes sufficient to prevent light or anything else escaping from its surface. This whole process—the death of a star—takes some millions of years—good news for the human race, as the sun still has some way to go before even starting this stage of its evolution. However, once, near the end of its life, it will explosively expand, so that any living creature remaining at that time on earth would be fried. Once its contraction phase starts, its density will steadily increase. All sufficiently large stars reach the moment, when, based on the laws of gravity, nothing should/could be able to escape from their surfaces, since nothing could travel faster than light. For, even for something travelling at the speed of light, the gravity of the dying star (if large enough) would have by now become sufficiently strong to prevent its escape.

Neither humans nor roebuck, even much earlier in this process, would have any hope of escaping its gravitational pull if they approached too near. Pressures at the surface would be sufficient to suck in and crush even a tank. So any reindeer around would have been very keen to keep out of range much earlier in the process, if at all possible. Heisenberg, in his 'Principle of Uncertainty', concluded that, nevertheless, sub-atomic particles[2] continue to enter and escape from black holes. He argued that they are able do so because the physical properties of the position and velocity of a particle - or for that matter, The Brig supposed, of a Reindeer - cannot both be measured at exactly the same time. The more precisely one property is known the less precisely the other can be known.

This is because it is not possible to measure precisely where a particle is at any point in time without it moving—for the very act of the measurement itself moves it. If you could establish precisely where it was when you started to measure its location, in three dimensional space, you could not then measure precisely what its velocity had been at that time; and, hence, where it was by the time you finished measuring.

"Like Wallace's squirrel", suggested Archie. The Brig thought what a remarkable intelligent insight. "Well, not exactly", he replied, "Although it is true that the very process of measuring its location is quite likely to cause it to move". He added that the converse was true too; for, given the precise velocity and direction of a particle at a given point in time, you could not know precisely its location at the time you made the measurement, for during the act of measuring its velocity, it would have changed location—again as most probably would have the Squirrel or even the Reindeer.

The Brig had to admit that it was unlikely that he would succeed in putting forward such a principle as an acceptable defense if he were to be caught by a laser speed trap travelling in his car faster than the laid down limit. However, following Heisenberg's Uncertainty Principle, a minute sub-atomic fundamental particle might be either inside or outside a black hole's exact boundary (known as its Event Horizon) at any given time. For these particles have this astonishing ability of being at point 'a' at one moment and at point 'b' at the next, but no one has ever caught them moving from one point to the other.

"They would be very good at 'Grandmother's footsteps", said Archie, intelligently. He was no mean hand at that game himself.

---

[2] *To complicate matters, these particles behave like waves when in motion though as tiny dots when still.*

"I expect so", agreed The Brig, smiling at the thought. "So", he continued "these particles are thereby able to seep or radiate out of the hole, as described in the now generally accepted Hawking Radiation Theory. In this, Stephen Hawking predicted that any star, once it becomes a black hole, will continue to shrink by emitting radiation (in the form of particles) and thereby reduce in size, to the moment when it finally completes the cycle of its life, a few billion years after its birth.

At this moment it becomes merely a point in space and then nothing; the nothing from which it began—thereby completing its life cycle. Archie was clearly puzzled by the whole concept, as was The Brig, if truth be told—and particularly uncertain about those particles and whether the Reindeer was an exception to, or example of Heisenberg's Principle. Wallace was just glad he wouldn't be around when the sun burnt out.

The Brig tried to simplify things. "Everyone knows", he said, with more confidence than he felt, "that there are two basic measurements to be made to locate any object on a flat surface (like a billiard table) relative to an already known object at any given time—for example, from the white ball to the black ball at the other end of the table.

You can measure the relevant object's distance from the white ball on a known bearing (say straight up the table); then you can measure the distance from a right angle from your line (i.e. straight across the table) to the black ball. This gives an 'x' and 'y' measurement, which precisely, in two dimensions, locates the black ball relative to the white ball.

For a three dimensional body, like a reindeer, there is also up and down (height or depth). For example, the reindeer might be 'y' yards to the left of the right angle from a given bearing, (call this measurement 'width'), 'x' yards from your location to the right angle to that bearing from you (call this 'length') and, being on a small mound, 'z' yards above the level where you were ('height').

So you could express the reindeer's exact location at that time relative to yours, in three dimensions, given a bearing, in terms of 'x', 'y' and 'z', feet and inches or meters and millimeters, dependent on your choice of measurement system. Its velocity is measured by the time it takes to move from point 'a' to point 'b' in terms of feet or metres per second". Wallace had by now moved off to sniff out a tuft of grass and Archie was struggling to keep up with The Brig, who however, relentlessly talked on, whilst continuing to walk at the laid down light infantry speed of 140 paces to the minute. Archie was beginning to think he was getting slightly more than he bargained for when agreeing to go on this walk. What was The Brig on about?. Why was he talking so fast? Why was he walking so fast. The stuff about the object on the billiard table really did bother him. Surely it was simpler than The Brig made out.

"Time effectively makes a fourth dimension, we call 't'", he continued, "for, the precise time the Reindeer was at 'xyz' from your location is also critical to his location, since he might well have— like the squirrel—moved on during the taking of the measurement. He might, of course, like those particles, move because of the measurements themselves, especially if a ticklish tape measure was used. Some eminent physicists additionally and confusingly predict", he added, "that there are an additional seven spatial dimensions across the universe, i.e. a total of eleven dimensions, but these extra seven, if they do exist, are very, very small and circular - you quickly end up where you started from."

Archie was hoping that they would soon return to where they started from. He thought about diverting The Brig to talk about the score in the Test match, or who England should open the batting with. But The Brig just added "They are really only of concern in Quantum Physics, dealing with minutely small fundamental particles, the ultimate building block of the universe and to scientists seeking their nirvana, the long sought after 'Theory of Everything'". Archie wanted to know more about this 'Theory of Everything'. He figured that if he could get hold of this concept it might just possibly make some sense of the rest of what The Brig was talking about, he optimistically hoped.

Meanwhile, Wallace had lost all interest in Mobjacks, in the as yet unsighted Reindeer, in Heisenberg, in black holes and in locating particles at 'x', 'y', 'z' and 't', all with no scent and no visible dimensions. He was certainly not prepared to hang around to listen ay more to this 'Theory of Everything', which was unlikely to reveal anything of concern to even the most intelligent dog. He had an acute sense that The Brig had lost his scientific bearing and began himself to daydream, imagining running through a field of corn, chasing a very beautiful Labrador....

The Brig stopped talking for a moment, as he dealt with Wallace pulling on the lead surprisingly hard, as though he had forgotten where he was. Although not unsympathetic to his lack of concern about this arcane area of science, he optimistically sought to try again to clarify the Theory of Everything.

"The aim of this theory, he said, "(which is, by the way, known as the 'Grand Universal Theory' or 'GUT', for short), is to unify in one single mathematical formula, the three now accepted theories of physics, each one of which is universally obeyed throughout the Universe These are the theories of gravity, of weak and strong nuclear forces and of electromagnetic forces". Before Archie could ask what these were, he hurried on, "So far, the only formulae found, which fits all the facts and combines the three above theories of physics, is the so called 'Superstring Theory', which assumes that all fundamental particles are tiny vibrating strings, vibrating in different frequencies across the universe. This theory, though mathematically neat, requires the extra seven aforementioned dimensions". Both Archie and Wallace were temporarily silenced. Concepts as weighty as time and space were being presented to them anew, concepts which required a lot of thought and patience to grasp. Although both were bright and inquisitive creatures, each, if truth be told, was relatively baffled as clearly was The Brig himself.

He meanwhile pictured these billions of unimaginably tiny violin strings, floating and strumming or vibrating like an orchestra across an eleven dimensional universe, visualizing to himself a sort of Beethoven symphony in space (or perhaps a night at the Proms, with Benjamin Grosvenor at the piano). Wallace was not keen on any loud noise—thunder, bell ringing and explosions of any sorts terrified him—so he hoped that, if this strange concept was right, the strumming would continue to be gentle. He glanced up from the grass he was chewing to see The Brig looking dreamily into the horizon, as though not altogether there, and surmised that he was probably imagining himself conducting a great metaphysical orchestra, or some other such grand vision. Wallace decided to enjoy the moment of peace while he could.

When The Brig enquired of Archie whether all this made any sense to him, Archie was honest enough to say that frankly it made little, if any! Archie was good like that. The third child of The Brig's son Jamie, he was a very intelligent young man, with an enquiring mind and a good sense of humour. He was honest as the day was long as well, and was unable to avoid telling the truth, even when others would have perhaps been a little more diplomatic. The Brig secretly rather agreed with him over this Superstring Theory. Although the formulae were mathematically irrefutable and neatly fitted all the known facts, it was still, he felt, one of those scientific concepts drawn up either by the sort of wild eyed person you would quietly seek to back away from—"sorry, very interesting but I'm afraid I've an urgent appointment elsewhere that I must attend"—or by a brilliant scientist.

This theory, at best, is a neat but still unproven and seemingly improbable concept, even given the evidence of the particle collisions recently achieved at CERN.

There was silence as Archie and, possibly, even Wallace, The Brig optimistically assumed, digested these pearls of wisdom. By now, they had almost completed the circuit through the woods. The Brig noticed that both of them looked relieved, although he wasn't entirely sure why. Perhaps the mud had made the walk more arduous than it usually was.

To finish the walk, they set off down the track which quarters the wood and descends gently back down to the car park. Archie was unusually quiet, whilst Wallace, with renewed interest, eyed the two approaching black Labradors—perhaps wondering if they were inside or outside the event horizon, though The Brig suspected more likely that his interest was more basic and noted with relief, that they were both on leads. Anyway, they were more attracted by the riders trotting past than Wallace and passed safely by without incident.

The car park was full. Skirting the assorted families and dogs milling around, The Brig unlocked his car and the three of them unhurriedly clambered in, bringing with them, he noted with resignation, a fair proportion of Bucknell Wood mud, picked up on their walk (along the various footpaths and streams which meandered through the Wood) and now generously deposited on the floor and on the seats of his new Volvo. Archie asked if, next time, they could do the Slapton to Abthorpe walk. Wallace's ears pricked up. This was one of his favourites, perhaps because he remembered the incident when he saw off that aggressive Rhodesian Ridgeback (of which more later).

Back home that evening, they (well, Archie and The Brig) listened to the weatherman, who forecast a period of sunshine over the following week. A walk to Abthorpe was accordingly agreed. So, the next day, they duly set off once again, driving from Wappenham to Slapton, the start point of this walk.

Leaving the car by the Church there, they took a back route through the village, to where a right-of-way footpath skirts an old mill house. As they passed by, the two large Alsatians, who lived there, barked furiously from behind the stout slatted wooden fence, which separates the millhouse garden from the footpath. Wallace deliberately, silently and provocatively, as he did every time he passed by, marked the other side of the fence. Infuriated, they redoubled their barking, running up and down the fence, as he jauntily, tail and chin up, strutted by.

From the Mill, the public footpath runs past some chickens in or around their pens, which Wallace disdainfully ignored, to a narrow arched wooden foot bridge across a fast flowing stream, which runs under the Mill. The bridge itself leads into a long rectangular field, which the footpath crosses to reach the embankment, which used to carry the now sadly long disused Towcester-Wappenham section of the London, Midland and Scottish (LMS) railway line.

As the three of them approached the embankment, The Brig nostalgically recalled the old steam engines, as they lumbered, snorted, whistled and puffed their way across the beautiful countryside, connecting villages and hamlets to towns and cities. In those days, the line, LMS—affectionately known as 'Long, Meandering and Slow'—connected Helmdon to Towcester and Northampton, via Wappenham and Abthorpe.

Wappenham, at that time, The Brig told Archie, remembering similar scenes from his own childhood days growing up in Wiltshire, had its own Railway Station, open from 8am to 6.30pm, with a Station Master (and Assistant Station Master to take over during the lunch hour!) The station itself boasted a general waiting room, a Ladies' Waiting Room, a Gentlemen's Waiting room, a Ticket office, a Cattle Dock and Sheep Pen amongst its several buildings. Often a dozen or so mooing cattle patiently waited to be driven to board the rear coach (behind which was the Guard van) on the twice daily train run, before it puffed its way out of the station, on its run to the Northampton cattle market. It all reminded Archie of 'Thomas the Tank Engine'. Like many of his age, The Brig still fiercely blamed Mr Beeching and the government of that time, for the closure of these lovely and locally valued country lines, for what was claimed to be a necessary saving in the then tight economic climate. Many today considered that this irreversible cut was remarkably short sighted in light of the line's value to those who lived in these otherwise rather remote villages spread across the rural countryside.

The Brig wondered if future generations might feel history had repeated itself, either in some of the harsh cuts being imposed today to reduce far greater deficit or, conversely, over the new high speed rail line (HS2). Like many living around the area, he had openly canvassed against the latter, which would cut like an arrow through the beautiful Northamptonshire countryside to take, what was argued by those against it, a mere thirty minutes off the London to Birmingham commute—in their view a dubious reward for its enormous and uncertain cost and the damage and noise it would inflict.

Others, of course, today argued passionately, like Beeching did those many years ago, of the undoubted benefits of the proposed plan. A new superfast line from London, through Birmingham to Manchester using 200mph trains would, in their view, be an important first step in developing such a network across the UK, thereby helping bring Britain out of the Victorian railway era and 'up to speed' with the rest of Europe.

They argued too that the then estimated £17 billion cost of the line to Birmingham and £30 billion to Manchester would quickly be repaid by the economic benefits of closing the North South divide. Listening to the news, it looked as if their arguments had prevailed. Archie was fascinated by trains and happy for HS2 or any other similar rail development to go ahead, but Wallace, who had never actually been in a train, clearly agreed with The Brig that it was a rotten decision. He was much happier with the beautiful open countryside and the smells in the field that they were now crossing. It was, as usual at that time of the year, full of sheep and lambs, with notices underlining an incident (involving the untimely death of a savaged lamb) that reminded owners that all dogs had to be kept strictly on leads.

As always, Wallace was smugly on his extending lead during this walk. However, he was not in the least bit interested in the sheep. He found them to be dirty, boring and stupid. They, nevertheless, moved sharply and warily out of his path. Trees, brambles and shrubs now grew wild over ground on which the track, removed long ago, once lay. The disused embankment now boasted, in lieu, a muddy footpath, which followed its old route, winding its way along the embankment. Following this overgrown footpath was hard going and potentially painful, with brambles and branches, but still possible, as The Brig and Wallace had painfully discovered on a previous walk. The fields on either side of the railway embankment were separated from it by stout sheep fences.

The right of way footpath gained access from one field to the other across the embankment by the use of two wooden stiles. These were equipped with ingenious dog flaps, which owners need to lift, to allow their animals to pass safely through, before (or after) they themselves climbed over the fence, using the steps on the stiles. Wallace casually lifted the flap with his nose and pushed on through, leaving The Brig to follow, untangling the extended lead.

The second stile led into another sheep filled field, the far side of the old line. There were then a choice of two right of way footpaths from there, one leading up to and through the village of Abthorpe and the other 'right flanking' the village across open fields, with three further stiles to be crossed to reach the top of the village. They took the latter option.

Crossing the much used Wappenham - Abthorpe road there (with care) into yet another field full of standing corn, they followed the footpath through the corn, to where, at the top of the village, it joined the Abthorpe - Bucknell Woods farm track, which itself shortly thereafter deteriorates into a muddy track, skirting the western edge of these woods. This right of way footpath then joins the farm track, which takes a sharp turn to the left through the village, before leading leads back to the old railway line. The full circuit, following this route, from the church at Slapton through Abthorpe and back to the church takes some thirty to forty minutes on foot, with a five minute additional but attractive diversion on the route back around the Mill House to the Mill Pond, to which they had taken Wallace, on an earlier walk.

He had found a rabbit track there, running steeply down to the Mill Pond. The Mill Pond was large for a country pond, fed by a sizeable stream, which first runs through Slapton (the village above the Mill), where it rushes noisily over a sluice gate, then drops down some ten feet into the churning waters of the Pond below. Connected to this main Mill Pond is a smaller pond, which Wallace found he could reach via the rabbit track; and then, lead permitting, jump in, to have what he felt to be 'a well-earned drink and wallow'.

When Wallace took to the rabbit track, The Brig's options were to check him half way down (requiring considerable strength, as Wallace was extremely strong, no light weight and desperate for a drink), or to undo his lead (which he was loath to do with the two now noisily barking dogs in the Mill House garden nearby) or, as a last resor,t to negotiate his own way down the rabbit track to a narrow ledge above another steep and muddy drop into the water below. He unwisely selected this last option.

Archie, who remained at the top, unintentionally tested The Brig's balance by reaching down, to touch his shoulder and ask. "Grandpa, what is a molecule?" "A good question Archie", The

Brig replied, rebalancing on the small, but somewhat slippery shelf, sweating slightly as he juggled the many challenges that currently faced him, while thinking Archie might have timed his question more carefully. "Everything you can see, feel or touch, including your own body and the muddy slope I am in danger of slipping off into the water below, is made up of atoms, forming elements, in turn bound together as molecules", he grimaced.

He continued, still checking Wallace and hoping not to himself end up in the Pond, "Each molecule consists of a cluster of elements. For example, amino acids (building blocks for living bodies from which you, I, and Wallace were all 'constructed') are made up of elements of Hydrogen, Oxygen, Carbon, and a smattering of other elements, themselves formed from atoms". "A water molecule", he reminded Archie and Wallace, as he continued to balance uneasily above the pond in which Wallace was by now happily wading, "consists of two elements, Hydrogen and Oxygen".

"What is an element?" Archie persisted. "An element is a substance that is made entirely from one type of atom" The Brig replied. "For example, the element Hydrogen is made from those atoms containing only a single proton and single electron". "Atoms", he added, before Archie could ask "consist of a nucleus made up of at least one proton (with a positive charge) and usually a neutron (no electric charge), circled by one or more electrons (with a negative charge). They are all very, very small, especially electrons."

"How small, Grandpa?" Archie predictably asked. "If 200 million atoms of Hydrogen were placed side-by-side, holding hands as it were, their combined diameters would be less than a centimetre and if the nucleus of an atom was the size of a golf ball, its electron would be half a kilometre away", replied The Brig, now with one gumboot in the water. As Wallace bathed, he noticed with admiration The Brig's commitment to answering these questions in testing circumstances. He decided to pull harder on his lead, to test The Brig's resolve further.

"An electron is nearly 2000 times smaller than a proton or a neutron. These latter two, however, are roughly the same size. There are some ninety naturally occurring elements, he continued, which vary in weight according to the number of neutrons, protons and electrons involved in their make-up. The heavier elements have more of these and the lighter ones have fewer. Helium has the least", he recalled. Wallace at last relented at this and The Brig helped him scramble up the bank, back onto safer ground.

"If you split an atom", he went on, slightly breathlessly, "you get at least one electron, one proton and usually a neutron or two. If you split any of these, you get a fundamental particle, which most physicists believe is the smallest thing possible in the universe. It is very, very small and can either be a 'lepton' or a 'quark'.

There are six types of leptons, including muons, gluons, taus and neutrinos. There are also six types of quarks (including up quarks, down quarks and coloured—red green or blue quarks), which group together to form 'hadrons'. A lepton and a quark are both particles. All hadrons and quarks have anti versions (made up of anti-matter) and all may appear in the form of these tiny vibrating strings, vibrating on high or low frequencies—like music". Archie looked stunned.

"Do you follow me so far?" The Brig optimistically added, as he continued to struggle to keep his balance and provide a coherent response to Archie's persistent and acute questioning. The latter politely indicated that he did not, but Wallace, by then shaking himself on the grass above the pond, with water liberally sprayed on his protesting companions, looked up nonchalantly, as if, of course, he did. The Brig felt that was just as well, as he would have found it very difficult convincingly to explain much more and was already, scientifically anyway, in deep water.

He was also still struggling with avoiding slipping into the pond and even more by trying to explain what he had read, particularly about hadrons and leptons. However, he was by now physically, if not scientifically, on safer ground. Back in the field and on safer ground, despite clearly having lost the interest of at least half his audience.

However, he doggedly and gamely continued:- "There are four types of forces in nature, interacting between these fundamental particles. These four forces, to remind you, are gravity, weak nuclear, strong nuclear and electromagnetic, as I outlined earlier in that so called 'Grand Universal Theory' or 'GUT'. Physics can be applied accurately to each of these forces individually, to predict the outcome of an event. For example, thanks to Isaac Newton's work on gravity, it is possible to predict the acceleration of an apple as it falls from a tree and its speed as it hits the ground, assuming that the height from which it fell is known". Archie, predictably asked what exactly was gravity? The Brig explained that it was best described as an attraction between two masses, the greater the mass the greater the attraction, but inversely proportionate to the square of the distance between the centres of the two. Gravitons are believed to be the fundamental particles which carry out this work.

The strength of the attraction, he added, thereby built up between two large stars of sufficient mass is, astonishingly, sufficient to bend light. Archie asked, hopefully, whether he too was attractive enough to bend light a little and whether his Gravitons attracted him to his friends. The Brig ad-libbed "Maybe, but only in a very small way. Humans have insufficient mass to have measurable gravitational attraction, although any mass, however small, is attracted to and by any other mass"

Given sufficient mass (that is, a sufficient number of Gravitons), The Brig agreed that light could be and, indeed, was bent this way, across the universe. He had even read of military research into bending light to provide a 'cloak of concealment' to hide objects such as warships.

"As I mentioned earlier", he continued, "scientists, until recently, had frustratingly been unable to reconcile Einstein's 'General Theory of Relativity', which states that gravity acts on space and time, with the 'Quantum Theory'. This latter theory deals with the nature of subatomic particles and sets out mathematical formulae to predict the effects of weak and strong nuclear forces, which bind protons and neutrons within the atom, on their structure.

The fundamental particles that do this work are called respectively bosons and gluons. One of the former is 'The Higgs Boson', sometimes named as 'The God Particle' – having been made famous following recent experiments at the CERN, the scientific research centre in Geneva. It, however, is not always, unlike God, entirely successful in its job, particularly when there are a large number of neutrons within the atom concerned. (In such cases, the neutron will, in certain conditions, give up or radiate out an electron and become a proton).

"Radioactive decay in nature", The Brig concluded "is an example of weak nuclear forces in action. Atomic bombs utilize the dramatic effect of breaking up strong nuclear forces. A 'gentler' example of electromagnetic force can be seen by looking at the way a compass will always point to what is known as magnetic North". Wallace immediately pointed north, possibly to let Archie know that he knew all about such matters. The Brig reminded the puzzled Archie and the now static Wallace, as he remained pointing north, that the Superstring theory is today the only mathematical formula that successfully integrates the effect of these three different forces.

"To complicate matters", he explained to his increasingly switched off and disinterested audience—though Wallace curiously remained frozen pointing North—"although everything you can see, feel, touch or smell in the universe is made up of these forces and particles (which join together to form atoms, which in turn form molecules, which then form different objects, including you and me), there is still a lot of stuff out there in the universe that you cannot see, feel, touch, or smell (even with the number of smell receptors in your acute nose, Wallace)". Wallace looked suitably impressed. The Brig continued, "Mathematicians have calculated that up to 96% of the Universe is made up of this stuff, now known as dark energy and dark matter, some 76% of the former and some 20% of the latter, leaving only some 4% that we can actually see, feel, touch, or smell."

"What exactly is dark energy? Is there light energy too?" Archie asked, adding that both he and Wallace had lots of energy, but no one had ever before talked to them about its colour. "Cosmologists", The Brig explained, "remain divided on this question and even whether dark energy really exists. However, without it, the universe would be unable to continue to expand and accelerate at the rate it is accelerating now away from the point where it began; and its acceleration would be a good deal less than it was a few billion years ago. This would have been, in the long term, really bad news for its inhabitants.

However, fortunately, recent observations from the Jodrell telescope have shown that the acceleration of the galaxies furthest away from us is considerably less than those nearer us. As our measurement of the acceleration away from the original 'Big Bang' location of those furthest away from us (because of the time it takes for light from them to reach us) is actually the acceleration they were achieving many millions of years ago, we can be confident but nonetheless surprised that the universe continues to accelerate away from where it started, faster now than then.

The problem for those scientists interested in this was to explain why, which is where dark energy comes in. Its existence is predicated on the need for the mass required to provide a gravitational effect to generate the measured acceleration of galaxies away from their start point and thus enable the laws of physics to operate as observed. Measuring the mass of all visible galaxies was quite a feat in itself, but already completed to mathematicians satisfaction, confirming that there is more than enough 'unoccupied' space for the necessary level of dark energy to occupy and thereby allow the galaxies to achieve this measured acceleration (which would require dark energy to occupy some 76% of all space).

Scientists have measured the matter they can observe, which would fill a bare 4% of all space, leaving 20% to be filled with dark matter (that is matter we cannot see, touch feel or smell and has no energy but enables galaxies to spin as they do). Without this amount of dark matter, they would not—or that is what we are asked to accept" Even Wallace looked dumbfounded by that.

The Brig, bit firmly between his teeth, went on "The residual unresolved problem is that scientists simply do not know what either dark matter or dark energy are made of, because they are both invisible and have no electric charge. However, they are hopeful that the particle accelerator at CERN, as described elsewhere in this book, will provide further observational evidence of this strange stuff[3]".

---

[3]   Seven brief lessons on physics - Carlo Rovelli

He finally, to the undoubted relief of at least one of his audience, concluded, "Scientists believe that dark matter enables galaxies to spin faster and provides the space for new stars and galaxies to be born, whilst dark energy accelerates the expansion of the universe to the level we can measure it as so doing." Archie muttered that all this stuff made his head spin. "Perhaps that is because it is full of dark matter", The Brig thought he heard Wallace reply. Archie, perhaps fortunately, didn't hear that aside. However, he remembered reading that CERN's recent work there, using The Large Hadron Collider, had provided credible evidence of the existence of dark matter, through the brief existence of relevant particles. Archie recalled that, in his computer games, dark forces always sought to annihilate the forces of light. "Is dark energy an evil?" he asked.

The Brig replied, "Probably not, since without it, the universe would cease to expand at an ever increasing rate and might by now already be contracting under gravitation forces; and on its way to ending up with a big crunch to form a massive black hole that would eventually radiate and disappear into nothing—a neat but unpleasant completion of its cycle from birth to death". "Perhaps", Archie replied, "a new universe might then form from this?"

"Good thinking, again", The Brig acknowledged. "That is indeed one of the theories put forward by some physicists. However, it looks as if the Universe can, by its acceleration (using this dark energy), escape that end for some while yet. Nonetheless, the majority of those today involved in research into the cosmos, accept that, as postulated in the fourth law of thermodynamics, without the expenditure of energy, everything over time turns to dust, or, in the case of the universe, into negative and positive particles, thus returning to the nothing from which it was formed.

"This fourth law predicts, in a slightly different way to that which I sought to explain earlier", The Brig concluded, "that the eventual end of our Universe, in a few trillion years (as, over these eons of time, each and every star will burn out its supply of hydrogen and becomes a black hole). Then, unless a sufficient number of new stars and new galaxies are born (and this would require sufficient (dark) energy), 'The lights of the Universe' would go out across the sky, and it would return to its start point 14.7 billion years ago, back to nothing".

This prediction of the end of our Universe, admittedly some trillions of years ahead, silenced Archie, though Wallace, still pointing North, took it in his stride as something clearly any Staffie worth his salt would know. "Though why on earth," Wallace said to himself (as no one else was listening—a problem The Brig often faced on their walks), "should anyone be interested in something that would not happen either in their lifetime, or even in the lifetime of the human or canine race. And why bother with things like dark energy", he sagely concluded to himself, "which no one can see, smell, touch or feel, particularly if its existence is only predicted by its observed effects, such as bending light and the speed that galaxies are moving away from the site of the 'Big Bang'".

With that snap conclusion, he rather smugly crossed the field ahead of his physically and mentally exhausted owner, as they made their way up the hill back to the car parked by the Church.

# Chapter 5

## *Dogs in Wallace's Life*

APART FROM THE FLIRTATIOUS GOLDEN Retriever who lay in wait by the lake on summer mornings, Wallace's three favourite 'girl' friends were Bramble, a good looking Springer Spaniel owned by The Brig's youngest son Digby, Wooflie, a Newfoundland and later Domino, a Vizla, both of whom had been acquired by his eldest son, Simon.

**Digby, Bramble and Wallace**

Bramble was athletic in build, well set up and superbly fit, and could squeeze into the smallest space. She often came up to Wappenham, curled up in the corner of the crammed boot of Digby's car, raring to 'go', as soon as they arrived. She soon became a good friend and companion for Wallace. As she lived in Fulham, with limited opportunities there for exercise (although Digby did have a 'dog walker' during the week and often went running with him), she particularly enjoyed the fields and wide open countryside of South Northamptonshire.

She loved tracking down and chasing wildlife there, particularly birds and squirrels. Given the opportunity, she considered chickens 'game' too, so needed to be kept under fairly tight control, when off the lead. She was a great hunter, very fast and would comfortably cover ten miles for every one of Wallace's. In the summer, she particularly enjoyed a swim in the lake down the hill from Wappenham. However, the year Bramble started coming, the lake had just been officially opened to licensed fishing.

As The Brig, Digby, Wallace and Bramble approached the lake on one hot summer Sunday afternoon, she dived straight in, to the consternation of some dozen outraged and vociferous fishermen, leaving in her wake entangled lines and vanishing fish, as she swam, in hot pursuit of some quacking and flapping ducks. Recalled eventually by her owner, with groveling apologies all round, she was thereafter kept firmly on a lead whenever near the lake. With her long hair, she collected mud easily in wet weather and needed a fair degree of drying off and cleaning up on return from winter walks before being allowed into the house. She was, however, a gentle and loving dog, who caused little if any trouble (other than of course the mud and hunted prey!), and The Brig much looked forward to her visits with Digby and his family. Although Wallace could not, even in his prime, keep up with her, he also was very fond of her and the longer and faster walks were good for his health, fitness and waistline too.

Wooflie was as 'black as the ace of spades'. She was a large Newfoundland, several times Wallace's size. She appeared in Wallace's life when he was a puppy. She belonged to The Brig's eldest son,

Simon and his partner Harriett and came up quite regularly on visits to Wappenham. Wallace, as a puppy, was entranced by her and would dash around trying to seek her attention by jumping up at this dog mountain. She generally ignored him, until he became too bumptious or flirtatious, when she would just sit on him. Not only was she very big but very strong!

The two of them soon became good friends. Some of The Brig's neighbors', who were a bit frightened of Wallace as he grew into a full grown male, were amazed to see this unusual couple trotting happily alongside each other across the local fields. Sadly, she died quite young. Simon then acquired a Vizsla, he called Domino. Vizslas are Hungarian Pointers, descended from an ancient hunting breed owned by Magyars, who settled in Hungary hundreds of years ago. Since then, these Pointers have been inbred with Weimaraners and German Short Haired Pointers.

The outcome of this breeding was, for Domino, a medium sized, handsome, deep chested, athletic looking dog, with a body covered in a short golden brown hair—similar in colour and length to Wallace's red coat. She was wiry, athletic, boisterous and strongly built, but with small eyes and a small head, and was unusually fast and energetic. She was friendly with all humans and sought to engender and then enjoy any knock-about game.

Domino loved coming up to Wappenham, with its miles of open fields to explore and the opportunity for some energetic games with Wallace, to whom she was clearly attracted. She enjoyed romping with him, ever since she, as an inquisitive puppy, first met him. She had been spayed, so had no interest in sexual involvement, though Wallace at times needed calming down at the point when games and wrestling lead to heavy breathing and panting over excitement on his part.

Outside, she was just too fast for him to keep up with, and like Bramble, covered at least ten times the distance he could cover in any given period of time. She enjoyed 'bombing raids', coming in at high speed at different angles of approach to a somewhat startled Wallace, to leap over him. At night, and if left in the house when the family was out, she would put up, uncomplainingly, with being shut up in her cage, though definitely pleased to be released the next morning and taken outside. More often than not, she accompanied The Brig, Simon, and Wallace to Farthingstone Golf Course when they went there, whilst she was up at Wappenham.

Provided the course was largely empty, she was released from her lead to exercise in and around the general vicinity, covering the ground at enormous speed. She was, however, well trained, so generally kept well away from other golfers and came quickly to heel when Simon whistled. Domino, like Wallace, was clearly very intelligent, but seldom stayed in one place long enough to join in any philosophic debate, except about her sleeping arrangements.

She had made it obvious that she would prefer Simon's bed or similar comfort rather than the cage; she thrived on human attention. Simon had a dog walker in London called Roger, with whom Domino spent much time. She was very happy with him and the long walks he took her on whilst Simon was at work. For, like all Vizslas, she craved both exercise and company.

Reflecting on relativity and the way time slows down as one approached the speed of light, The Brig wondered by how much it slowed for Domino, as she hurtled across the countryside, in full flight. When she spotted Wallace's squirrel in the garden, it was forced to race, with heart pounding, in order to reach the safety of the nearest tree with Domino's jaw's only a foot or so away, at a speed, which seemed to observers to be approaching that critical speed when time actually stops.

Embarrassingly, a couple of chickens from the farm next to the Old Rectory were not so fast, nor so lucky, when she found a hole in the fenced hedge bordering the two gardens; and chased, caught and killed two of them. Fortunately, the relationship between The Brig and the Farmer and his Wife next door was good; and groveling apologies and offers to purchase the corpses were respectively offered and declined. The fence was hastily raised a foot or two and repaired and Domino firmly constrained when in the area of the farm and their remaining free range chickens, whose eggs The Brig continued to purchase—at the a very reasonable price!

Watching her graceful and fluent movement—poetry in motion—as she covered the ground in full flight, a safe distance from the farm, he reflected on her role in life. Darwinists would argue that one of the main purpose of any species' existence is to propagate more of their species. But Domino has been spayed, so would never have puppies. So, if this rather depressing view were to prove correct, there would be no longer, in Darwin's factual world, any compelling purpose to her life. The Brig however considered that to be a relatively one eyed point of view. She gave pleasure and enjoyment to all whom she met and her beauty added to the great canopy of brilliance and experience that was life on earth.

The Brig suggested to Wallace that, perhaps, her more spiritual role was, for a few years, to be a companion and friend to Simon as he, like all of us, struggled through the complexities of life. This reminded him that sadly Wallace, to his knowledge, had never had any offspring either. However, if the sole role in his life was to provide love and companionship for a lonely old man, The Brig felt he had succeeded beyond God's wildest dream. And if she and Wallace were sometimes willfully disobedient, he hoped that such minor misdeeds would not count against them on judgement day and decrease their chance of promotion in their next life. Wallace was very attached to her and would, undoubtedly, given the opportunity, point out that many of the human rules she disobeyed were pretty stupid anyway.

It was clear from the look on Wallace's face whenever Domino was near that he would very much like to be able to catch up with her and ask her what she thought about things. She was, in his view, a very attractive and entertaining friend. Despite Wallace's unwelcome reputation, particularly when young, for threatening other male dogs, his main quarries, throughout his life, were actually the ugly black cat from a house on Rectory Way, the grey squirrel in the Old Rectory garden and rabbits and roe deer on or around golf courses. He never had the speed to catch any of them, but, given the opportunity, much enjoyed the chase.

His arch enemy was the garden squirrel that inhabited The Brig's garden at his house at Wappenham, who, in the autumn, could often be seen brazenly digging holes on the lawn. When spotted and chased by Wallace, the latter would amble to the nearest tree, climb up to a suitable branch, just out of reach and, balancing provocatively, sneer down at him. Wallace rarely barked, except when a stranger approached the house or on sighting this cheeky squirrel, though he howled dismally when the bells of Wappenham Church were rung, as they regularly were on Thursday evenings.

He had no fear of anything but loud noises, like gunfire, fireworks, or thunder, all of which transformed him, even as an ageing adult, into a trembling wreck. He never really learnt to cope with these terrors. When a thunderstorm passed overhead, it was painful to watch his reaction. Indoors, he would creep under any shelter or into the nearest cupboard; and if outside, pull very hard—and he was extremely strong—in the opposite direction to the noise. Hearing the blast of a nearby shot gun, he would shiver with fright, as if remembering a past incident. The Brig was convinced that in a former life, Wallace must have been shot at and hit, perhaps by a farmer, possibly chasing sheep, though that is something he never did in this life—and indeed never showed any interest in them whatsoever. Unlike Bramble, his great friend, who, given the opportunity, would, unless checked, hare after them and round them up, Wallace regarded them as too stupid to be worth bothering about. Cows were different. He still liked to stalk or face them down, though he wouldn't actually chase them.

Some years before Wallace's birth, The Brig had become a member of a nearby golf course close to the village of Farthingstone. Wilson had been admitted as an honorary guest and routinely came round the course with him. Wallace, as it were, stepped into his paws—the two look much alike, both being Staffies and The Brig suspected the Golf Course Committee just assumed Wallace was Wilson and so he continued to enjoy Wilson's 'golf membership' and even allowed, at The Brig's discretion, off his lead.

He loved his walks there, particularly on hot sunny days, when he could, divert to one of the many ponds on the course for a wallow and a drink. He was not the least bit interested in the golf itself or in anything useful like finding balls, but kept a sharp lookout for foxes and roebuck. In good weather, he usually waited patiently, loosely held on the extending lead clipped to The Brig's golf bag as the latter addressed the ball, following equally patiently as the former searched for it, after a not unusual slice into the woods. Wallace was not, however, a foul weather golfer and if it was cold and wet, would attempt a sit down strike in the hope of being taken back to the car. He had to be dragged by his extending lead a sufficient distance to realize that it was better to put up with getting wet than getting half strangled.

He often met an unusual friend at The Farthingstone Golf Course—a surprisingly agile three legged Spaniel, who was also allowed there as another member's dog. The two got on famously— unusually as the Spaniel was male—and would greet each other warmly, before Wallace set off to follow The Brig around the course.

However, there was one memorable, and less welcome occasion of Wallace and a spaniel, at the prestigious New Zealand Club, where The Brig's Charity, (The PSP Association) ran their annual fund raising event. The New Zealand Club is a well-known and up-market golf course—around which Wallace had been allowed, on a lead, to accompany The Brig. Whilst the latter was addressing his ball on the sixth tee, Wallace quietly bit through his lead and set off with the clear intent to rough up a large 'male' Spaniel he had spotted earlier, now also on the course. The two had met at the Club House, when it became quickly clear that they had taken an instant dislike of each other. After a few snarls, they had been separated, but this was a second opportunity Wallace felt he could not miss.

As he approached the Spaniel, The Brig's son, Simon, moved swiftly and caught him by the collar in the nick of time to prevent a potentially awkward and embarrassing situation. Apologising profusely to the owner, they withdrew, Wallace firmly back on a spare lead. The time had come to lay down the law. The Brig eyed him sternly and asked him what he had thought he was up to. Wallace returned his gaze with a look of pure innocence.

The Brig could read his thoughts, which were something like this. . "Well, Dad, whilst you dragged me around the course, stopping at intervals to hack a small white ball from tee to green, I was driven, mainly by boredom, to nibble through my lead". "You've never done that before", The Brig replied crossly. Again he could interpret Wallace's response. "I was just seeking the necessary freedom to investigate, greet and, if necessary, challenge that ugly brown and white spaniel I met earlier at the clubhouse, where we had exchanged some strong views on pecking order". His message was, "no harm intended, Dad, I just wanted to put him in his place".

In any debate about acceptable behaviour, there are three criteria for judgement. What was the intent of the offending party—in this case Wallace—at the time? What rules are necessary for a society (on a golf course) to cohere? Did the offender break or intend to break these? There was perhaps a fourth consideration too. At a higher level, what did the conscience of those concerned inform them about how they should behave?

The Brig coldly informed Wallace that (i) biting through his lead, whatever the provocation, was unacceptable behaviour; (ii) it was clear too, to all, that he was intent on confrontation and probably engagement with the Spaniel; (iii) no dog was allowed on the course unless they were on a lead and properly behaved; and (iv) although he could not be sure of what Wallace's conscience was telling him, he suspected that it was advising him strongly against his action. He should know that any repetition of such behavior would almost certainly result in him, and probably The Brig too, being banned from the course for life; and certainly for him to be left back at home or in the car next time. Suitably admonished, Wallace trotted dutifully behind him for the rest of the game.

Walking peacefully up the eighteenth hole, Wallace waited patiently for his end of game biscuit. After the last putt, he accordingly looked up hopefully for his usual reward, but The Brig was in no mood for bribery. A sadder and hopefully a wiser Wallace followed him back to the car with all the dignity he could still muster, cold shouldering the smug looking Spaniel as he walked past him at the entrance to the club house. Like all Staffies, Wallace's genes and breeding reflected both their fighting instincts and devotion to 'their human family', sharpened and honed as a puppy prior to meeting The Brig.

A loving family, training and preventative measures, had reduced the risk of Wallace becoming involved proper fight. This was the second occasion, however, of what could have become a nasty incident, and very embarrassing for his owner. It certainly lead to an at least temporary estranged relationship between The Brig and another dog owner. The first had been, when he had had a hostile encounter with an aggressive black Labrador. He had rushed up in the field to say "hello" to this large mountain of an animal and was immediately attacked and bitten painfully—judging by his squeal—on the shoulder. He retaliated fiercely.

The Labrador's owner and The Brig eventually managed to separate the two, but Wallace bore a mental, as well as a physical, scar to remind him of the incident; and thereafter would, given the chance, challenge, on principle, any black male Labrador he met. He had had to be taught, and learn the hard way, that, in a human's world today, neither fighting nor attempts at instant sex were acceptable behaviour, however much he was provoked or tempted! Fortunately, Wallace never did any serious harm to any opponent, and major scuffles were mostly avoided. However, it was, each time, on three occasions, during his life, very awkward and unpleasant for those involved. Wallace never fought with a dog smaller than himself, except when attacked by a brave Highland Terrier, who, thereafter, kept well away from Wallace, whenever he spotted him. Unfortunately, this Terrier lived nearby in the same village, so avoidance tactics were called for and successfully applied until the Terrier returned safely to Scotland a couple of years later.

These incidents during Wallace's younger years did neither his, nor The Brig's reputation in Wappenham much good and meant the latter felt he had to keep the former on a lead at all times outside the Old Rectory's secured garden (and, for a probationary period, to Wallace's disgust, actually muzzled in the village). Meanwhile, The Brig booked him in for some serious 'dog training'. Barney, a black Cocker Spaniel a month or two older than Wallace, lived just down Rectory Way from The Old Rectory and had been Wallace's best friend, when they were both puppies. They had then scoured the countryside together as young pups in search of game to chase.

Barney's owner and The Brig used to go for long walks together, with the two young dogs chasing rabbits and hares; playing energetic games and having mock fights.

About a year later, however, there started to become an edge to their games and, sadly, it eventually became necessary to keep them both on leads and apart. They retained, however, a delicately balanced friendship until Barney's owner, David Foden, a good friend and near neighbor, suddenly, sadly and unexpectedly died from an embolism after a hip operation and soon thereafter his wife, Jo, and Barney moved to London to be near her family. Barney had, up to then, been Wallace's best mate.

Soon thereafter, The Brig and Wallace had visited his son Jamie and his family in Wiltshire on a beautiful sunny Saturday morning and parked his car in their drive. Jamie had a lovely and spacious Georgian manor house in a beautiful village called Heddington, which lay beneath the Ridgeway as it cut through South Wiltshire. Jamie met them at the car, and confirmed that his dog was shut up. No animals were believed to be around. Wallace was grateful to exit the car off his lead after the long journey from Wappenham.

As he did so, The Brig spotted, to his horror, Jamie's then young daughter, Honor, open the front door accompanied by her new kitten, which calmly sat down by the entrance to lick her whiskers. Wallace immediately eyed the kitten and before he could be arrested, set off toward it, gathering momentum rapidly over the gravel. For the observers, time slowed right down. As he closed in on the kitten, it made no move to escape. The Brig pictured one bite and one dead kitten; and a major family rift. He saw Honor, a favorite granddaughter, and the kitten just standing there. There was nothing he could do but shout a warning to try and prevent the imminent but apparently certain disaster.

And then, the kitten, showing all the balletic brilliance for which her race is known, looked up. Just as Wallace was seemingly on her, she nonchalantly stepped to one side, extended a paw to clip Wallace across his nose, drawing a drop of blood, and leapt nimbly onto a nearby window sill, out of reach. Wallace could not stop in time and crashed into a pottery ornament, cracking it, then on into the house wall. It was a work of genius and Honor's kitten sort of smiled as she saw Wallace in a comedic heap next to the house.

Wallace turned round, looking rather dazed, as The Brig and Jamie ran up, with a slightly embarrassed, apologetic smile on his face and blood dripping from his nose - realizing he had been made to look very foolish in that encounter. All The Brig could feel at the time was immense relief.

Some six months later, The Brig, accompanied as usual by Wallace, once again drove down to see his son Jamie and his family. Jamie had, by that time, acquired Otto, a large and friendly black Labrador, so, knowing Wallace's views on Labradors, care had to be taken to keep the two apart. Meeting his Father in the drive, Jamie confirmed that Otto was shut up in the boot room and suggested Wallace might like a quick run around the garden off the lead, before being confined to the car (with a later walk up the nearby hill). The garden was secure, with a gate and cattle grid at the entrance.

So The Brig let him run free out of the car. Wallace set off happily around the garden, sniffing and smelling the rose bushes and lawns and marking 'his territory. Meanwhile, one of Jamie's children had found Otto shut up in the boot room and decided to let him out. He naturally came over to investigate the arrival of a strange new male dog in his garden. Their meeting inevitably and very quickly turned into a fight and Wallace soon established a grip on Otto's loose skin and fur near his neck before eventually Jamie and The Brig succeeded in separating the two. The Brig then took the disgraced Wallace back to his car and shut him in the back for the afternoon.

Otto fortunately had only minor cuts on his neck and ear, but thankfully nothing life threatening. Nonetheless, it was an extremely embarrassing incident, although Jamie's family were generously forgiving. All the same, after that, The Brig kept Wallace on his extending lead or in his car (in the shade with windows opened sufficiently wide for plenty of fresh air, but not sufficient for use as an exit) whenever visiting them. Surprisingly the ageing Wallace and Otto settled down to a friendly coexistence during the many further visits thereafter. They often quite happily went for walks together on the Wiltshire Downs, with Otto running free and Wallace trotting along on his extending lead. They appeared not the least interested in fighting each other again and neither did they ever do so, much to everyone's relief.

Safeguards, such as leads and avoidance procedures had accordingly been built into Wallace's routine, balancing quality of life and levels of freedom with a reduction in risk of a fight. Over the following seven years, Wallace managed, with the help of his training, his extending lead and other control measures imposed by The Brig, to keep a clean sheet.

For the record, there was one further incident, when Wallace was the innocent party, walking, on a lead with The Brig, in an open to the public field near Slapton, was approached from some hundred yards away at speed by a young Rhodesian Ridgeback, by itself and not on a lead, who rushed up and immediately attacked Wallace. After a short sharp engagement, Wallace had locked on the Ridgeback's neck. A long minute later, the Ridgeback 'surrendered' and, after the two had been separated, his young owner, very shaken, took him off. Fortunately, there being no visible damage to either participant, other than loss of pride, they all were able to continue on their respective ways.

One of The Brig's—and Wallace's—favorite combination walks was in central Towcester, where the former could do his weekly shop at one of the three supermarkets, which this small Roman Town boasted, whilst Wallace guarded the car. After the shopping, they would walk along an unexpectedly attractive municipal footpath (recently installed by the Council and replaced, at no little cost) followed by a broader less attractive pebbled track along which a truck could then drive.

This track runs alongside a stream, past housing estates to the fields beyond. Two schools for young children, a playground and a considerable number of assorted dogs with their owners makes this an interesting and potentially eventful walk. Although Wallace's occasional urge to fight with other male dogs had been considerably reduced by training and time, his interest in the opposite sex had definitely not! Passing aggressive male dogs and attractive female bitches now led, however, to no more than mutual interest, with, for the former, some tightening of leads and for the latter, their potential entanglement.

Wallace retained his 'eye for the girls' throughout his life and demonstrated very direct interest in any 'lady dog' he met, often, to be fair, reciprocated, as he was still a very handsome male; and so, the retracting lead was needed to restrict romance to a friendly greeting.

As they moved off to the car and drive home, The Brig had to admit that this fighting instinct was in human as well as canine blood, though there were obviously different rules for men and dogs. The former make what the latter might feel to be somewhat arbitrary decisions on what is a just cause and about the difference between a freedom fighter and a terrorist. Wallace accordingly asked himself whether there were circumstances and, if so, when, it might be acceptable for a dog, too, to fight another dog? Self-defense was a case in point. If attacked, retaliation using reasonable force, was, in his view, clearly justified, but was it, in any circumstances, acceptable for either dogs or humans to attack first—a sort of pre-emptive strike in retaliation to a threatened cyberattack? On such issues, The Brig reflected, we all tend to draw our own lines; though a dog, perforce, needs to adhere to human's social judgements and rules or they, and probably their owners too, risk paying the penalty.

Following this logic, in the case of the Rhodesian Ridgeback, Wallace was clearly within his rights to counter an uncalled for attack; but in the case of the aborted attack on the Spaniel he was equally clearly not! Wallace was well aware of the laws of the jungle and the rules of the wolf pack and from his experiences with humans, some, if not all, of their, to him, not wholly consistent rules on fighting, and, by then, generally accepted both. As a thoroughbred Staffie, pride prevented him from ignoring a challenge by any equally powerful opponent and, given the opportunity, he was only too happy to demonstrate his fighting superiority. However, throughout his life, after his first fight, he was both constrained by his lead and other preventative measures and, now as he aged, his obedience levels were considerably higher than when young. That is probably true for most of us, The Brig ruefully reflected.

That summer, he and one of his sons, Richard, were going for a week together a World War 1 Battlefield Tour in France; and planned to take Wallace. This visit to the First World War battlefields and cemeteries; and the ongoing debate over whether, and if so, when fighting between humans—let alone by dogs—was ever morally right and if so when, is discussed further in the next Chapter.

# Chapter 6

## *Routine and Not Going Abroad*

AFTER A WALK FROM HOME, Wallace would normally lie at full stretch, head between paws and legs extended behind him on a small but long settee, in the Old Rectory, where he would contemplate life. This settee was located strategically by the hall window, viewing across the front lawn onto Rectory Way, a small lane beyond. The Brig liked to think that Wallace was analyzing the key points of their most recent philosophical debate, though recognized that it was more probable that he was watching out for any movement on the lane and/or assessing information gleaned from the scents collected during his morning walk.

Occasionally, he would sit up and stare intently out through the hall window onto Rectory Way, observing people, dogs, horses, cars and the occasional lorry passing by. Dogs, people, rubbish collections and paper deliveries were particular highlights. No barking, just intense excitement and a visit to check whether anything had come through the front door letter box. Anything that did was assessed for 'value'. Wallace had his own system of assessment and would give short shrift to 'advertisements' and junk mail posted in. He very occasionally 'got it wrong' and tore open a letter or notes of importance. When he did, the Sellotape came out and he was made to realize his mistake with painful penalties, such as the denial of his morning biscuit. (There was, perhaps fortunately, another mailbox by the door of the outbuilding, opposite the back door, which the postman.at that time normally used).

All dogs, and most humans too, like routine. Wallace's best days included his early morning walk, a quiet period on the settee, then around 10.30am, a mid-morning game, followed by a biscuit and short siesta before an outing in the garden and lunch. In the afternoon, his favorite occupation was a short drive, preferably to the nearby and much loved Bucknell Wood, followed by a good walk, then home, with in the evening some squirrel chasing in the garden, followed by his main evening meal and, in winter, a doze beside a log fire before bed.

A change of routine or worse, 'going away', as all dog owners know, can be quite stressful for both dog and owner. The Brig suspected that Wallace read his diary as, even before a suitcase was sneaked out, the latter was suspicious and alert to being left behind. As the time to depart approached, even if it was obviously just for a few minutes, he made it clear in good time, by his assumed demeanor of unutterable misery, that he was keenly aware of his approaching abandonment. If the Brig took him with him, as he did whenever he reasonably could, even if it meant hours in the car, Wallace was overjoyed and lay by the door to the back drive, where the car was parked, his tail going back and forth like a metronome.

If not, once the suitcase was out by the back door, he would go sorrowfully into The Brig's study and lie there awaiting his fate, head between paws, in quiet resignation. He didn't move when The Brig finally came to say goodbye and depart—just one reproachful look, which spoke far more than words of treachery. A sneaky exit through the back door invariably left The Brig feeling those dog-associated pangs of remorse and sadness. However, a few moments after he had gone, Wallace would quickly cheer up and settle down happily with his in-coming house/dog sitter. He knew and liked them all. No kennels for him!

The main three – Jenny, Ann and the third, surprisingly named Cat —were all by now good friends of his. Although he would often not eat for a day or two (quite good for his overall shape) and mope around a bit to add to The Brig's guilt in abandoning him, food and walks, with whichever one of his 'sitters' was there, would once again restore him to an outward appearance of enjoyment of life. Whilst away, The Brig would make a routine telephone call or two to check all was well; and meanwhile worried unnecessarily about him, for all three carers' were not only extremely capable but very fond of Wallace too.

Wallace had been born and registered in the Kennel Book, with - as mentioned earlier - the unlikely name of Kara's Red Flame, on 27th April 1998. His identification chip No. 41432F2A2C was inserted at the Towcester Veterinary Centre on 16th March 1999. On 29th May 2003, he acquired his Pet Passport GB120344 on completion of his required Nobivac rabies injections. He was, from then on—provided his documents and injections were regularly updated, able, under the then EU rules, to travel from the UK across Europe.

At about this time, The Brig's third son, Richard, took up a job based in Geneva; and the idea of a visit to Switzerland, accompanied by Wallace, was mooted and reached firm planning stage. The Brig had found out on his earlier visit to see Richard in Geneva (which he sneakily combined with a short skiing holiday), that he could drive to Luton Airport (less than an hour's drive from home) leave his car at the midterm parking there, walk to the airport, catch an early flight (6.30am) and be in Geneva, where Richard met him, just before 10am local time. The two of them then had driven on to Verbier in Switzerland, in time for a late lunch and some afternoon skiing. However, such a winter visit for Wallace would not really have worked—and not just because skiing was on the menu.

Indeed, with only a small stretch of the imagination, The Brig could picture Wallace hurtling down the mountain on four short skis—probably better at accelerating downhill than traversing or stopping. He was certainly, when young, keen to have a go at any such outdoor challenge, particularly when the sun was out. He had made it clear that snow was great, but he did not much care for the cold. Flying out for him, however, was not really a viable option, even though pre booked dogs in transit are welcomed by most airlines. Wallace would have objected most strongly to (and been quite upset by) being put in a cage in the hold for the flight; and his processing through customs at Luton and Geneva would have been, to say the least, fraught. The alternative of driving out meant an extra day each way and probably an overnight stay in the centre of Geneva, with no nearby long grass or other canine facilities immediately to hand (except in a fine manicure and hairdressing salon next door to Richard and Louisa's apartment, patronized by rich Swiss poodles and other similarly well cosseted creatures). The reluctant conclusion was that a winter visit accompanied by Wallace was not really on, but a summer one was still a possibility.

There are far fewer restrictions for dogs in Switzerland than in the UK. Restaurants, for example, usually welcome them as well as their owners and, even in central Geneva, there are plenty of parks and lakeside walks. However, taking Wallace abroad—even to mainland Europe—would still present quite a few administrative headaches, not least the detailed paperwork and necessary veterinary clearances once there to enable him to re-enter the UK. Eventually The Brig decided, the following summer, that such a visit was all just too difficult and that it would be best if one of his friendly house/dog sitters looked after Wallace back at Wappenham, particularly on long weekend visits to Switzerland.

Despite re-examination of this decision over the years, it was not until 2009 that, once again, a visit for Wallace across the Channel became a realistic possible starter. For The Brig and Richard had that year agreed to do together a World War 1 Battlefield Tour in France, in the Amiens/Arras area. They would, this time, definitely take Wallace!

The Brig accordingly checked and updated Wallace's passport, rabies injections and relevant papers and booked a car/rail channel crossing for both of them that June from Folkestone to Calais. He briefed Wallace on the plan, during a walk a week before departure. Richard would take the train from Geneva and The Brig would pick him up in Amiens. He accordingly contacted and made arrangements for the two of them and Wallace to stay at a friendly hotel near Abbeville (including dog sitting arrangements), whilst in France.

The idea was for them to overnight there for three nights. Each of the first three days, they would visit the battlefields around the

Somme and then, on the fourth day, drive on from Arras out to Vimy Ridge, before returning to Calais. The War Graves Commission confirmed that well behaved dogs on leads were entirely acceptable to them. Both The Brig and Wallace were quite excited by this plan; and a detailed itinerary was worked out, together with a route plan. Wallace was naturally keen to help in the viewing of the large scale map, which The Brig had assembled and spread out on the floor at The Old Rectory, covering that part of Northern France where they would go. Accordingly, he made a close personal investigation of the area, though was briskly called off to prevent any attempt to mark enemy trenches.

The Brig and Richard agreed that they would first drive around the countryside and villages where the July 1916 Somme Offensive had taken place. They - and Wallace too—then wanted to walk some of the battlefields and visit the beautifully kept World War 1 and 2 cemeteries there. They also agreed, before leaving the area, to drive along the general line of the Canadian and Australian forces advance from Amiens in 1918. About a week before setting off, Richard learnt that his job in Geneva would require him to be in the UK for a meeting immediately after their Battlefield Tour and suggested that a more efficient plan might be for him to drive from Geneva and pick up his Dad in Amiens.

That obviously made sense, but it meant Wallace, once again, would have to be left behind. For it would have been extremely difficult for The Brig to take him, by train, across the channel to Amiens and, even if he managed that, Richard's car was much smaller than his—the two of them plus their luggage would leave little room for a large Staffie and his sizeable accoutrements. Once again, the news had to be broken to Wallace that he would have to stay behind. As always, he took such news with calm resignation, metaphorically shrugged his shoulders—what would be, would be! So, on the agreed day in June, The Brig drove off, leaving a rather miserable looking Wallace in the house with Jenny.

He left his car at as secure location in Milton Keynes, taking a fast Virgin train from there to Euston, where he boarded Eurostar for Folkestone and, from thence, under the Channel and on to Calais.

Changing trains in Calais, he was then taken on a secondary line across the rolling countryside of France via Boulogne to Amiens. After a brief tour of Amiens Cathedral and an anxious wait back at the station, he finally, with some relief, met up with Richard, who had been seriously delayed by traffic around Paris.

They overnighted, as planned, in an impressive Chateau near Abbeville, with peacocks strutting around its well laid out gardens. The Brig had a vivid dream that night, in which Wallace, in the Chateau's gardens, was in hot pursuit of a peacock. He was grateful to wake up and realize the dénouement he feared, was but a dream. Leaving the Chateau each day after an early breakfast, they spent a moving—in every sense—three days, touring World War 1 Battlefields.

Their main focus was on the Somme offensive. This offensive was planned and reluctantly undertaken on 1st July 1916, by the then Commander-in-Chief of Britain's Army in France, General Haig. Reluctantly, because he felt that the raw British troops to be committed, needed much more training first. He had eventually actually planned this offensive to take place in mid-August, but was persuaded, by the then pretty desperate French Commander-in-Chief Joseph Joffe, to make a much earlier start to relieve the almost unbearable pressure on their forces around Verdun.

Haig's plan relied on, what was then, for the British Army, a novel massive rolling artillery barrage to destroy, or at least soften up the defenses sufficiently to allow his main infantry advance to overwhelm the German lines. His overall objective, the taking of which he was quietly confident, was the high ground between Peronne and Baupaume. Once again, in hindsight, the over optimistic assumption that the pre-planned rolling artillery bombardment would at least temporarily incapacitate or destroy the German machine gunners and forward trench systems and cut through the barbed wire that protected them, proved to be tragically wrong.

Because the mass of infantry used in the assault were raw untrained recruits, they were required by the plan to move forward from their trenches strictly in line abreast, at one hundred yards every three minutes (to conform with the barrage), each carrying some 60 lb packs on their backs. The assault was, in the event, a massacre, as advancing troops were first stopped by the wire, then mowed down by the largely undamaged German machine gun emplacements.

At the end of that day and, indeed over the next week's fighting, there was little in the way of ground captured to show for the immense British (and Allied) effort despite the courage shown and lives lost. The largely abortive push did, however, achieve a key part of its objective in relieving pressure on the French at Verdun; for the Germans were forced to throw in reinforcements to hold the line against the persistent and determined British attacks, thereby weakening other sectors. However, the price was high. Overall, in the Allied offensive on 1st July 1916, there were some 54,470 allied casualties, of whom some 19,240 were killed.

Richard suggested that, whilst they were in the area they ought to drive to Beaumont Hamel, a small village nearby, which they duly did. This was where the Royal Newfoundland Regiment (recently assembled from young men, recruited in Newfoundland and then transported to France), had been sent 'over the top' in an assault on German defensive positions, at 8.45 am on Ist July 1916.

After a massive artillery bombardment to destroy the wire and soften up the German lines, little opposition was expected. It was some 300 yards, slightly downhill across bare open ground, from the Newfoundland trenches, to the well dug in and camouflaged German positions. In the event, only a handful from the Regiment, under intense fire, made it to a lone tree three quarters of the way across the open ground toward the machine gun manned German trenches. 733 of their total strength of 1044 men, including 22 officers, had been killed or wounded in less than twenty minutes. This devastating loss represented the majority of the young men of fighting age from that then small Dominion of the British Empire, now part of Canada. The beautifully kept memorial with a bronze Caribou and the War Museum there are moving memories, for these Newfoundlanders and their families ,of that terrible morning.

The Brig and Richard found driving through those villages strung out along the beautiful Somme countryside and, particularly walking their battlefields, very moving. Being there with the sun shining and peaceful silence and walking over green and pleasant fields made it difficult however to imagine the bare brown landscapes, the tree stumps, the shell scrapes and the endless rain softened mud of these battlefields together with the noise, confusion and chaos of those days in 1916; or fully appreciate the raw courage of those involved, particularly those young soldiers, burdened down with their packs, as they struggled courageously forward through the mud and the barbed wire entanglements in the face of murderous machine gun fire, in that terrifying and terrible assault, so movingly reflected in the nearby cemeteries. These immaculately kept cemeteries, with their row upon row of tombstones, many just inscribed 'Known only unto God', reflected somberly on the appalling loss of life on both sides, including the flower of the British Empire's youth.

Leaving the Abbeville Chateau on the fourth morning, Richard and his Dad then drove North and East from Arras to Vimy Ridge, captured by the Canadian Corps from the Germans in fierce fighting in April 1918. This assault was part of the Allied Arras Offensive, the final great battle of World War 1.

The capture of Vimy Ridge was part of a brilliantly planned attack, mainly carried out by tough battle hardened Australian and Canadian troops. Their great offensive and the arrival of American troops, in fact, led directly to the German collapse and resulting Armistice on 11th November 1918.

Richard and The Brig left the area sadder and wiser men shocked by the waste of young lives but moved by the courage and determination of those involved. The latter wondered what Wallace would have made of it all.

En route back to the channel ports, they diverted to visit Agincourt and view the scene of the battle that had taken place there some six hundred years earlier, when Henry V, together with his knights and longbow archers, had, on St Crispin's Day 1415, defeated a much larger French Army. Walking across the fields to where the English army and archers had been drawn up for battle, the two of them looked down the slope to the stream, to where the French knights and their horses advancing up the hill, had been mowed down by the longbow arrows of the English archers. From this field, it was a short drive to the nearby museum.

This well-kept French museum displayed an array of longbows, arrows, cross bolts, Madam Tussauds style archers and knights, with personal armour and other battlefield memorabilia. It also offers an excellent and gripping film—a reconstruct of the battle (in both French and English) -which vividly and, it has to be said, generously, depicts the full extent of the French defeat.

Leaving behind Agincourt, they approached the outskirts of Calais, and, with a couple of hours in hand before their cross channel train departed, they diverted from their direct route to the Channel Ports, to visit the V2 museum at Wizernes, just outside St Omer. This museum is located in the bowels of an old quarry, which had been carefully selected by the Germans, in 1943, to become a 'hardened' long range rocket launching site.

Wizernes was one of their main fixed (as opposed to more successful mobile A4/V2) rocket sites. The site had been constructed, using some 40,000 forced labourers in under two years, to provide, under a massive reinforced concrete dome, deep within the quarry, anti-aircraft batteries, a storage facility for the rockets to be brought in using a rail spur, a protected launching pad and housing for some 200 to 300 personnel. The complex was completed in 1944, by which time the Allies had identified it as a key target for air attack.

In a series of such attacks, some 3000 tons of bombs were dropped on or near this key target, mostly with little effect. However, in July 1944, a Lancaster Squadron raid using 6 ton Tallboy deep penetration bombs, effectively damaged the site to such an extent that no V2 rocket was ever successfully fired from it again. As a result of such raids, only those V2 rockets fired from mobile sites were successfully launched to hit London and other morale damaging UK targets.

The museum itself was competed in the 1970s. Although The Brig felt Wallace would have enjoyed Agincourt more, he and Richard found their tour of this complex so fascinating that they cut their time left to check in at Calais much finer than they had intended. During the resulting exciting drive to the coast, with Richard at the wheel, The Brig kept his eyes uneasily on the speedometer and kept a sharp lookout for police and speed cameras, sensing that they were probably travelling at somewhat above the French speed limits for that road. They were certainly moving pretty fast—fast enough in the latter's mind, for, as Einstein forecast, time to slow right down. In the end, they arrived breathlessly at Calais to be the last to board the train before the gates closed.

Arriving at Folkestone some thirty to forty minutes later, they had an easy drive up the M2, M25, M40 and A43 back to Wappenham, where they received a wonderful greeting by an overjoyed Wallace, with yet another touching display of enthusiasm and warmth. Once settled in back home, they showed him their route on the by now dog-eared map, pointing out the battlefields they had visited. Wallace showed what seemed to be considerable interest in all this, making a close inspection of the Somme, before finally sitting firmly on Normandy. Moving him gently off the map, The Brig, thinking of the wanton carnage of all these bloody battles, felt a description of some of the fighting would be of some interest to a Staffie like Wallace. After all, his ancestors, like ours, had been put into battle against opponents they neither knew nor personally disliked.

For those young Staffies in mining villages in the 'Black Country' were, a little over a hundred years ago, trained to face opponents selected arbitrarily (usually by size and ability), to fight to the death, in Staffordshire cellars, with sizeable bets being placed by the baying crowds on which dog would win. In some ways, The Brig couldn't help thinking, that was not that much different, for the young dogs involved, from the young men, like those from the Newfoundland Regiment, who were recruited and, when the time came, ordered to attack similarly aged German soldiers in trenches across a field from them, over which they must advance and kill or be killed. Although 'circumstance of where they are placed, rather than the moral rectitude of what they are doing that dictated their response. When faced with killing 'the enemy', whether it be a seventeen year old they transfixed with their bayonet, or a veteran they blew up with a shell, ten miles away, he felt, perhaps cynically, that 'Thou shalt not kill, *except when your Government so authorizes'* could be a realistic amendment to one of the Ten Commandments.

Soldiers are, of course, specifically trained to close with and kill or capture their opponents. The Brig's mind turned first to Afghanistan and Iraq, then Kohima in Burma, where in the Second World War, British and Indian soldiers, with immense courage, fought to the death with young Japanese men in hand to hand battles, with shells and mortar bombs raining down, arbitrarily killing or wounding those within their paths.

Any soldier, to be effective, needs to believe in his cause—as did many Germans and Japanese—but the moral responsibility for the death of those they accordingly kill rests, at the end of the day, with the Government that authorizes them to do so. Hence the need for Governments, The Brig concluded, (nodding wisely to himself, Wallace observed), before declaring war, carefully to balance their legal and moral responsibilities.

However, he recognized that any comparison between what happened in the trenches of World War 1 or on and around the tennis courts of Kohima and what happened in the cellars of houses in the Staffordshire coal mining area was not a fair parallel to draw and any attempt to do so was likely to cause offence at least to some. He wondered what Wallace thought about it all. "When dog fighting was, if not strictly legal, commonplace in some parts of the UK", he asked him accordingly, "how do you think the consciences of those responsible for organizing such events squared up with what they were doing in the name of sport; and how do you think those Staffie's felt?"

Wallace's view was, as always, pretty straightforward. He admitted he knew nothing of the organizers, but if he had been trained to fight and put in a cellar to confront another male of similar size, let the best dog win. That was in his blood. However, the fight, in his view, would be about who was the strongest and most skilful fighter. In the small number of 'engagements' he had had with other dogs, he had lived by this maxim and had shown who was best, but luckily with an only superficially damaged opponent! The bucket of water thrown at his face to make him let go, was, in his view, like seconds in a boxing ring or the referee separating the fighters. His own few scraps, he insisted, had, of course, just been to establish ranking! Nevertheless, if The Brig had taken him to Agincourt, he would have been happy to demonstrate his fighting skills to any selected French poodle, with or without referees. Having been left behind at Wappenham, he regretted missing that particular opportunity to prove himself in battle but would be happy to offer himself as a contender, against any combat ready French poodle or warlike German sheep dog.

Unexpectedly, another chance did arise for him to cross the channel—though, perhaps disappointingly for Wallace, fighting a poodle or sheep dog was definitely not on the menu. The Travel Agents involved in the battlefield tour planning had been, not unreasonably, unwilling to give a refund either for The Brig's booked car channel crossing or for Wallace's ticket. However, they did offer, to reschedule, at no cost, the crossing dates to any date not yet fully booked over the following six months, including a replacement crossing for one dog—a generous offer, in the circumstances, that could not easily be turned down!

The Brig therefore planned a channel crossing with Wallace in September, when The Brig, his cousin Stephen Frewen-Laton and his son Simon, all agreed to drive over to L'Escale near Le Touquet, together with Wallace, to visit the area and play a few rounds of golf. Once again, a dog loving hotel was booked and necessary veterinary checks were carried out.

However, yet again, at the last moment, there was an unexpected hitch. Frustratingly for Wallace and for The Brig—who couldn't help noticing that neither his son, nor cousin, seemed quite so put out by this development as he was—none of the Golf Course Committees in the area would allow dogs to accompany players around their respective Courses, so he had, yet again, apologetically to explain to Wallace that, regrettably, he would not, after all, be coming with them on this holiday.

With just one look of resignation, Wallace crawled from the study to his basket. The message was clear. He knew by then that he was destined never ever to go abroad! Fortunately, Jenny could come and look after him, so after an uncomfortably early start from Wappenham that Saturday, The Brig set off, on his own, to pick up Simon and Stephen at the latter's house near Tenterden in Kent, before going on to the Channel Terminal at Folkestone. Soon after setting off, he noticed a red light come on, on the car's dashboard display. Stopping at a lay-by, he checked. The oil levels were very low. So att the nearest garage, he bought a litre of oil, filled up the car's oil tank and checked the dipstick. The level was at full. Everything appeared OK. However, some ten miles later, the red light came on again. He put more oil in. Once again, after a few miles, the light came on yet again. He then assumed, wrongly as it turned out, that there was an electric fault at the gauge, and drove on regardless.

On reaching Tenterden, the temperature gauge was only just above normal, so, with his cousin and son, plus golf clubs and suitcases on board, he drove the last twenty miles to Folkestone. Arriving at the channel crossing to check in, he switched off the, by then, a very hot engine and went to the kiosk to have their papers checked. On his return, the car simply would not start. Meanwhile a queue was building up behind them. The Channel Crossing breakdown team were alerted and, after some discussion, the car was ignominiously towed to a nearby car park in the terminal secure area. A brief check, confirmed that the oil level had dropped to a very low level. They called the AA (The Brig was luckily a member). Some ninety minutes later, long after the cross channel train had left, the AA breakdown team arrived. They found, looking under the car, that its oil pipe, which led to the sump, had split, and the engine oil had simply steadily drained out on the motorway, during the journey.

The AA helpfully confirmed that The Brig's car engine had fortunately not actually seized up, but despite temporarily repairing the oil pipe and refilling, the oil pressure remained at near zero. They accordingly offered, as part of the service, to tow the car to any garage in the UK. Sadly, The Brig, after examining the alternatives, nominated his Volvo garage back in Northampton as the best location for the broken down car. The family were then escorted (with the contents of the car—including Wallace and three golf bags and assorted suitcases) out of the Terminal by the AA and dropped off at a lay-by to await the arrival of an outsize taxi they had ordered to take them back to Stephen Frewen-Laton's house.

After cancelling hotel accommodation in France, they drove in Stephen's car to Littlestone for a morale lifting round of golf there before returning to his house for the night. The next day, Simon drove, in his car, Wallace and his Father back to Wappenham, the latter suffering a mix of worry about his car and disappointment that the drive to France and their golf had had to be cancelled. The Brig still optimistically hoped to cross the channel with Wallace one day. However, the latter, he suspected, was by now resigned to the reality that he clearly would never ever travel overseas during his lifetime.

Back at Wappenham., one of Wallace's favourite walks was around the Silverstone racecourse, which lies about five miles from the Old Rectory. The Brig was not a particular fan of watching car racing (though he wouldn't, when younger, have minded having a go at the racing itself!) So, on known race days, he kept well away from the area, particularly during Grand Prix week, when South Northamptonshire becomes a magnet for motor racing enthusiasts. They would come in their thousands, on foot, on motorcycles, in cars, in buses and even in helicopters, all converging on the various routes which take them to Silverstone, noisily close by. (The helicopters bringing richer spectators and perhaps racing drivers, appeared to be routed directly over St Mary's Church, Wappenham, an obvious landmark right next to The Old Rectory).

Even on minor race days, particularly in the summer, the crowds build up and the high pitched noise of the cars or motorcycles hurtling around the track was clearly audible several miles from the circuit, (including, when the wind was blowing from the East) from The Old Rectory in Wappenham. Archie, on a visit, was, however, extremely keen to watch a race there, though the snarling of engines, the squeal of brakes and the overpowering smell of burnt rubber and overheated oil were all, in The Brig's eyes, major disincentives from doing so on the course and he personally would have preferred to watch this admittedly exciting sport on television.

Rather than queuing to obtain the necessary tickets required to watch from the quite expensive stands and leaving Wallace at home, The Brig suggested a compromise. They could drive to nearby Whittlebury Golf Course, leave the car there and follow an attractive right of way, which would take them past one of the fields abutting the race course, where a mound had been built up from which they could watch, from what The Brig felt to be a suitable distance, high performance cars or motorcycles appearing and disappearing, like toys, on the distant track, as they raced around the circuit.

After a short walk past Whittlebury Hall, the right-of-way track skirts Silverstone Racecourse, leading to a large wood some mile or so from the circuit, through which The Brig, had often walked with Wallace before. It brings you out fairly close to The Silverstone Course itself, as it climbs back up the hill., with,, on its immediate right, the Whittlebury Park camping and picnic area fields and, just beyond them, a large lake.

A camping area there, is, particularly on racing weekends in the summer, fully populated by enthusiastic motor sport addicts, with tents, caravans and cars.

On the lake beyond this campsite, moorhens, ducks, geese, and stately swans swim agitatedly, clearly put out by this invasion of their privacy, paddling frantically away from this activity close by. The Brig, Archie and Wallace carried on past them up the track, through gates marked 'To the race course', before entering the field abutting the wired off course itself. There they climbed up a grass mound, helping a reluctant Wallace up the quite steep slope to watch, at a safe and legal distance, the racing cars, by then in action, circling round the course

Chasing hares or mob jacks or smelling out the badger lairs would have been, Wallace felt, far better entertainment than watching noisy cars in the distance, from a cold and rather exposed piece of high ground. Archie, however, fascinated by the sight of these racing cars hurtling round the circuit, was keen to remain and declared he was definately going to be a racing driver when he grew up. Wallace made it obvious by a withering look what he thought of that idea. Stung by the look, Archie muttered something, which clearly didn't go down well with Wallace, judging by his expression.

The Brig hurriedly suggested they move on. From this mound, there was a stile onto to a road. By turning sharp left there, it is possible (and legal even without a ticket) to follow some way around the perimeter of the race course, before a right-of-way track branches off from the road to the left, taking one through a large metal kissing gate and along the left hand side of the circuit back to Whittlebury Golf Course and it's car park, the club house and a practice golf range.

A well exercised but still clearly upset Wallace was left at the Car Park guarding the car, whilst The Brig and Archie took a few clubs to the range to practice their swings. It was Wallace's turn, they felt, to meditate. On their return, some half hour later, Wallace was still clearly not happy, sitting bolt upright on the driver's seat. The Brig suspected that he was continuing to harbour some degree of resentment over Archie's remark, which he had perhaps interpreted as an unjustified and an unfavourable comparison of the respective intelligence of man and dog.

Wallace, to be fair, was a very intelligent dog and knew it. He recognized, however, that the size of his brain was somewhat smaller than that of the average human; and had learnt that intelligence was in some way related to brain size. For The Brig had once read out to him an article claiming that, in the next decade, some babies would be born outside the womb, using artificial insemination techniques, in order to enable them to have larger heads—currently limited in size by exit space—and hence greater intelligence. Wallace was also aware that the internal organization of the brain and the number of neurons therein—as expressed by our genes—played a major role in any assessment of intelligence. Quoting from 'Google', The Brig had explained to him that the average human brain contains some 100 billion neurons. Elephants and whales, perhaps surprisingly, were quoted as having a similar number, but cats quite a bit less. He had then had to inform Wallace that there were, according to Google, fewer neurons that a cat in an average dog's cerebral cortex.

Wallace was sure that those who supplied this information must have slipped up there, perhaps accidently leaving out a zero or two. Anyway, he reasoned, such figures are, at best, estimates assessed by humans for an average member of each species, and he was definitely well above average. He nonetheless had looked upset by what had been, he was confident, a careless mistake by Google.

After an uneasy pause, Archie predictably asked "What are neurons, anyway, Grandpa?" "Neurons", The Brig explained, pleased that the slightly hostile silence had been broken, "are electrically excitable (nothing to do with temperament, he hastily added) cells that process and transfer information by electro chemical signalling, via connections—called synapses—with other cells.

However, for neurons to transfer information, our brains have first to make decisions (using the same neurons) on proposed actions, such as whether to fight or to flee. "Wallace pictured the flow of neuronal instructions required to enable a Hungarian Vizsla like Domino to twist and turn and leap over him at full speed. The power and capability of a dog's brain in controlling such movement, even at his admittedly lesser speed, was, he clearly felt, truly awe inspiring.

Statistics comparing intelligence of man and dog were, anyway, Wallace reasoned, based on certain assumptions, which, in his view, very much favoured man. He would certainly not have accepted some of these assumptions, particularly those concluding that cats were more intelligent than dogs. (He couldn't, however, forget that embarrassing incident with Honor's kitten).

Wallace had also heard about that astonishing process known as apoptosis, when selected neurons are ordered by the brain to commit suicide. For all species are born with a large surplus (perhaps that was how the excessive number for cats had been calculated, he surmised), many of which, under instructions coded into our DNA, obligingly carry out these orders.

"This process is", The Brig explained, "important in achieving the correct location of neurons as they spread across the brain, so those that end up in the wrong place and those, which find there is no space left for them, are thereby eliminated. For babies as well as for puppies, this essential but deadly process happens in the womb, before they are born". "A bit like musical chairs", Archie suggested.

"Exactly" said The Brig, "but it is not just the size of the brain nor the number of neurons therein—though these are major factors—that dictates man's superior intelligence levels, but his ability to communicate through language skills and make sophisticated 'tools' such as computers, that gives him the edge over other species". Wallace clearly had reservations about that statement.

"However, The Brig hurriedly continued, quoting the eminent neurologist, Professor Colin Blakemore, "in order to do its biological job of sustaining itself and its genes, any animal must act as if the world exists for the benefit of it and its family alone. Our arrogance is to assume that we (that is the human race) are unique and radically different from the rest of the animal world. For all species are unique. If they were not, they would not be independent species". Wallace appreciated this assessment.

There is considerable evidence, The Brig reflected, that all species anyway share a common ancestry; humans from a line of evolution shared with chimpanzees. Still further back in time, it was a simple self-replicating chemical, called ribozyme, that initiated life of any sort on earth. Evolution, over the following millions of years had then led to many different life forms, with different assessed levels of intelligence. The Brig and Archie agreed that assessing intelligence was a difficult, subjective and ongoing exercise, though their conclusions on the comparative intelligence of different species and different members of certain species clearly diverged from Wallace's!

As the three of them sat in silence, The Brig concluded that genetic evolution and brain size were keys to the number of active neurons in the brain, which in turn largely dictated intelligence. This conclusion clearly left neither Archie nor Wallace entirely satisfied. They both remained quiet—the former probably still thinking about becoming a racing driver and the latter more likely about lunch. As they approached Wappenham, Archie suddenly asked "Who tells these neurons what to do?" This was a much more difficult question, The Brig felt. Wallace, he suspected, would probably simply say, in his case, "I do". To a large extent he would have been right, but, there were many underlying questions to be resolved before a more satisfactory answer could be given to Archie's acute query.

Questions such as how is 'I' defined and what factors go into making a decision that the neurons then act on; and what part do they, the neurons, play in this initial decision making process? And to what extent are such decisions hard wired and how much based on previous experiences? What role, if any, does conscience play? How much time is there to make such decisions and instruct the neurons how to action them?

"To take a simple example", The Brig observed, "a batsman facing a fast bowler may have less than half a second to decide on the line and movement of the ball and to make a decision on how to deal with it. If to hit it, there needs to be a series of processes involving locating, assessing speed and probable course of the ball, deciding on whether, and if so, where and when to strike it and, of course, passing on the necessary detailed instructions to the muscles of arms and legs to achieve the given aim. All this has to be done consciously and/or sub consciously in a fraction of a second".

He suggested to Archie that maybe the estimated two pounds of grey matter in a human brain controlling all this was astonishing. Wallace felt cricket was a pretty pointless game, but catching a ball in flight with his teeth was, in his view, at least an equally impressive feat. He could have added that a dog's reaction was far quicker than a man's and, according to recent research on canine intelligence, even a dog of average intelligence is at least twice as capable as a two year old child. A test for humans' intelligence, using a methodology designed by a dog, might even show the latter to be a lot smarter than that too!

Humans have some five million scent receptors and most of us think we are pretty good at sniffing things out. Who cannot, for example, recall the delicious smell of bacon and eggs, the whiff of a car's exhaust, the scent of a rose in bloom or more vividly, nostalgic odours, perhaps in the air on a cold frosty morning, or perhaps evocatively from the ozone blowing off the sea.

Yet a dog has some fifty times the number of scent receptors of the average human. Their sense of smell is phenomenal. Watch as they suck in, like a vacuum cleaner, that odour in the grass, their legs braced and attention absolute. At that moment, it is apparent that nothing else in the whole wide world matters. Concentration is absolute. What information is there for them to glean? They will have recognized the species of animal, its breed, sex, age and health and, importantly for a male like Wallace, whether amongst all the other information gathered, the provider of the scent is of interest or even 'on heat'.

With all those sensory receptors, The Brig suspected much more too, watching the care Wallace took in placing his 'mark' exactly in the right place from that endless capacity he seemed to retain (even after the longest walk, he never ran out). It was also interesting to observe the care he took in selecting the spot and the different cocking mechanisms used for making a mark than for relieving himself. The angle of attack and tilt for the former was much higher.

Dogs are also gifted too, The Brig reflected, with an astonishing sense of hearing. Wallace's was exceptional—a sort of mix of extra sensory perception and acute sound identification. In the morning, he often, as he aged, continued to lie at full stretch on the bed, whilst The Brig went down the stairs, tidied up the kitchen and engaged in other boring routines. However, within seconds of hearing the lock tumble at the garden door, some distance away, he would trot down the stairs and calmly appear, all ready for his morning walk.

The Brig regularly played tennis on a court in the garden some fifty yards from his house. When the players arrived, Wallace greeted them individually. However, he patently had no interest in the game itself and none in the tennis balls, so would then retire to the house and curl up on the spare bedroom bed upstairs, if he thought he could get away with it.

During the game, he was always somewhere in the house, dreaming or just contentedly sleeping. However, the moment the game ended, he would, with uncanny timing, re-emerge from the house and trot up to the court, to greet the players. Could he really hear, some fifty yards away, when the balls stopped being struck? And if so, why did he not come out at the end of a set, rather than at the end of the match?

Looking pleased with himself, tail going round like a windmill, he would greet exhausted players in turn, seeking an opportunity to offer a friendly lick, whether in commiseration for the losers and congratulations to the winners or because he likes the salty taste of their sometimes sweaty legs is a moot point—probably a mixture of both. Thanks too to his genes, Wallace, like other dogs, had remarkable eyesight. He would pick up a movement at a distance that a human needed a good pair of binoculars to spot. He would then stop and point indicating the direction of what he had seen to The Brig. Far quicker reaction time than humans was another asset handed down to animals genetically.

Wallace much enjoyed a regular morning game, when he would demonstrate his prowess and reaction speed. The question "Where is your bone?" would set him off in a search through the house of his imitation bone, usually left on the floor in one of the downstairs rooms. He would quickly track it down and invite anyone to take it from him. As your hand was about to grab it, he would move it just enough to make you miss. He had never once, over many years, failed to evade The Brig's grab, nor yet bite him, though, as the latter tried to grab the 'bone' he often put his hand in or near Wallace's mouth. Wallace's reaction time was astonishing.

"What", said Archie, "is reaction time". The Brig offered him an example for him to try on his friends. "Place a twenty pound note between your fingers, like this; then drop it without warning. If your friends, with their forefinger and thumb say an inch apart and half an inch below the note, can catch it as it drops, before it falls to the table or floor, tell them they can keep it. If not, they must give you ten pounds. You would make a steady profit with this trick, for most people's reaction time is far too slow! If they do succeed in catching it, they will either have cheated, been extraordinarily lucky or shown a quite remarkable and unusual reaction time, but still far, far slower than that of a dog.

In terms of intelligence, everyone knows", The Brig reminded Archie, "that computers are getting faster and cleverer. But they are not only getting faster but getting faster, faster. Moore's law states that the capabilities of computers will continue to double each year. They are already beating human in chess and other mind games. As their computing power increases along this exponential curve, artificial intelligence is expected to overtake organic—human and animal—intelligence by 2045, surpassing by then the combined brainpower of all human brains in the World. This future moment in time is known as 'Singularity', when the ultra-smart machines then available will have not only overtaken in every field that of the cleverest man, but that of the combined brain power of all human brains".

Archie, who was no mean hand at computers, knew quite a bit about this. They discussed who would then be in charge and whether man would seek to morph into these machines, initially with implants of computing chips, leading to a cyber-organic species. Meanwhile, Wallace wondered whether, with suitable implants, cyber dogs might perhaps overtake humans in intelligence. Archie liked the idea of a cyber dog. However, as The Brig pointed out, although computers were already able to store a phenomenal amount of information and were incredibly quick to provide answers to any question, they weren't so good at posing the question itself. So, how would a computer work without input from the human race? This question happily temporarily silenced both Archie and Wallace. They drove home quietly, each wrapped in his own thoughts. Archie was off back home the next day. Despite their differences over comparative intelligence and racing drivers, Wallace would miss him greatly, particularly on their morning walks.

# Chapter 7

## *Assessing Risks*

THE BRIG, ARCHIE AND WALLACE were lazily debating the future, in the garden, enjoying the warm summer sunshine, the morning before Archie's departure, listening to news on the radio about the potential effects of the rapid rise in the world population to over seven billion. Some more pessimistic scientists were forecasting that soon there would no longer be sufficient resources on earth to sustain its ever increasing population.

The Brig thought of those scenes in the Horn of Africa, with disease and death stalking the land, triggered by shortages of food, water and energy. He worried about whether Archie and his generation would have to face similar hardships as they grew up, with many of them expected to live to be well over a hundred (unless those more pessimistic scientists were right and their time on earth was cut short by, disease, famine or war). How would they deal with the growing number of emerging risks, such as that of a terrorist placing a dirty bomb in the cellar of a house in a city like London, or a rogue state using a nuclear weapon on its neighbour or an irresponsible and desperate Government authorizing the bio-engineering of a virus to spread death and destruction amongst its enemies?

And how would they cope with the potentially devastating effects of global warming? Greed and growing inequalities made for increasing, and potentially more damaging, risks to the survival of life on earth for humans, The Brig also wondered how as yet unborn Staffordshire Bull Terriers would fare. For they—like other animals—would have to face the potential consequences of human population explosion and possibly climate warming too. They were, he reflected, likely to face much higher levels of risks than the present canine generation; and what about the next generation after them?

To him, the future, a century ahead, looked very uncertain, Wallace, however, showed little concern about the next day, far less the next century, as he rolled on his back, with legs in the air, enjoying the warmth on his indelicately exposed stomach. He may indeed have been reflecting that in the foreseeable future, the canine species as a whole would not do so well, but, if so, he successfully concealed any concern he may have felt. Archie was, typically, much more worried about animals than about humans; and expressed the view that for those creatures lower down the pecking order, life could become pretty stark.

"Without food and water, you die", he reminded Wallace, who, having missed his morning biscuit, indicated he was well aware of that obvious truth. He had, however, always been well supplied and—without much effort on his part— provided with these essentials of life. Archie remembered Kipling's 'Jungle Book', which described how 'kill or be killed' was one of the laws of the jungle and reminded Wallace that animals in the wild already, daily, risked their lives daily to hunt and, if necessary to fight and die for food and water.

"Loss of habitat", The Brig added, "as 'their' land is cultivated or otherwise exploited by humans for agriculture, housing and factories, is already reducing the ability of many animals across the world to survive, except those in controlled and designated areas, such as nature reserves or, for the increasingly less wild, those, bred for consumption, put in a zoo or trained by humans to work to earn their living."

The Brig then, looking pointedly at Wallace, as he continued rolling unconcerned on the grass, added, "There is, of course, another way for a privileged few animals to survive, in some comfort; that of accepting the risks and rewards of life as a pet. This sharply reduces concerns about welfare and daily meals", he reminded Wallace, whose meat came from Towcester's best butchers. "There are, of course", said Wallace quietly to himself, "some less attractive consequences of being a pet, such as loss of freedom and a raft of penalties for not obeying imposed laws. For domesticated animals have to live within (if not always obey) the rules set by their 'owners even sometimes including castration'

Wallace had so far successfully avoided this particular assault on his manhood. "My main point, however", The Brig hurriedly continued, as Wallace carefully examined his lower parts "is that from birth to death, life is, at all times, uncertain and full of risk and these risks appears to be growing". Wallace, satisfied that all was in order down there, looked unperturbed by that thought and continued to enjoy the sun on his chest. Archie looked a bit embarrassed and confused, particularly about risk.

The Brig recognized that he needed to simplify the debate. He thought back to those years when he was young. "When I was your age, Archie", he began. "That was a very long time ago, Grandpa". Ignoring the innocent but painful interruption, he firmly continued, "When I was young, conkers were the thing". "But Grandpa ---, another interruption—"playing conkers can be dangerous. You might get hurt". Well, there was that risk, he thought, though it had, all those long years ago, seemed a pretty trivial one, particularly when compared to the risks in the war we were then fighting with Germany.

In more recent times, statistical and mathematical assessments of risk have led inexorably to what many of those of The Brig's advanced years would derisively call 'The Nanny State'. To be fair, he felt that many of these new laws were probably actually necessary, if only to ease the workload in our overstretched NHS hospitals. He reminded his audience that these laws were designed to reduce risk, minimising unnecessary accidents and deaths.

Legislation to enact such laws, like enforcing the use of seat belts in cars or prohibiting the use of hand held mobile phones whilst driving, though initially opposed by many, were now generally accepted (though speed cameras and related fines were still seen by some as more to do with some Council's stealth tax than accident prevention). "The important thing to balance here", The Brig pointed out to Archie, "is the risk involved in the individual doing or not doing something they want to do; and the potential cost or danger to others in their doing it.

Those ignoring imposed laws, by, for example, playing conkers at school or, as an employee, climbing a ladder over six foot, without a licence, (only to be issued following the necessary training and certificate), or contravening some other seemingly petty new Health and Safety laws, often fail to recognize this potential knock-on effect." At least a few of these laws, Wallace felt, thinking of some of the 'not allowed' rules he lived with, remained difficult to follow and even at times, he admitted, tempting not to.

The Brig reluctantly agreed there were some that frankly appeared to be stupid. For example, if, as a good citizen, you cleared snow and ice from the pavement outside your house in inclement weather, a passing pedestrian could sue you if they slipped and fell (and would be encouraged to do so by 'no claim, no fee' lawyers, seeking damages on behalf of their clients). However, if you didn't bother, they couldn't! Conversely, if a child slips and hurts him or herself in the playground in inclement weather, the school, in this litigious age, risks being sued by angry parents, so the playground is closed and children kept in their classrooms or sent home".

Archie said that when it had snowed the previous winter, his school had taken them out into a field with a steep slope to go and toboggan. Wallace loved the snow but with his short hair, he hated the cold. Archie mentioned that he had been reading a book about 'Scott and the Antartic'. "What and where is Antarctica, Grandpa?", he asked. "Antarctica is the continent which surrounds South Pole", The Brig replied. He continued, "It is approximately twice the size of Australia, but covered by a layer of ice on average over a mile thick, which is slowly melting and moving North toward the Continental Ice Shelf and the Atlantic Ocean.

It is the coldest, driest and windiest of all continents, with temperatures recorded as low as minus 80° C, averaging minus 25° C in midsummer. Katabatic winds, reaching storm force, batter the frozen mountain ranges surrounding the South Pole. Even for polar bears, it is an extremely hostile climate. For Staffies like you,

Wallace, with your short coat, to be located there, even for a few hours in the winter, without special protection, would certainly be a death sentence". Wallace shivered at the thought. "From March to September", The Brig added, "there is no sun. The rest of the year—between October and February—it is low on the horizon but, except during blizzards, still visible 24 hours a day. There is neither darkness nor night during these six months. Temperatures rise to an average of minus 25°C, but warming in midsummer (in December) to 5 °C near the coast"

Wallace shivered again at the thought of that biting cold, but Archie, to cheer him up, said that he had read that all the ice there would anyway all be melted by the end of the decade, due to global warming. The Brig mentioned the fairly recent setting up of a Research station close to the Pole, where painstaking measurements were being taken daily, by concerned scientists, of temperatures and of the rate the ice was melting in the area. He concluded, "Fortunately, their measurements indicated, fairly recently, that of only an average rise of temperature of no more than half a degree centigrade there over the last decade. Not all that much, though of more concern, there are some indications that it is increasing in rate. Moreover, in 1985, scientists had identified a large hole in the ozone layer above Antarctica, caused, they believed, by chlorofluorocarbons or CFCs (used then for refrigeration but now banned by International Treaty). This hole, which fortunately was believed to be now slowly closing, enabled ultraviolet rays to strike the earth's surface in the exposed areas around the pole, thereby warming and melting ice.

The sun's rays, when they fall on the sea, are absorbed, thereby raising its temperature. However, when they fall on snow, it being white, they are reflected. This means that as there is less snow, there is more water and less reflection. This in effect steadily speeds up the melting process. But it is not just this that was causing concerns about Climate Warming. The carbon dioxide levels emitted in production of the rapidly increasing levels of energy required in heating, lighting, motoring, flying and in modern manufacturing across the World, was increasingly believed, by many, to be steadily raising the World's temperature.

There is also concern", he added, "that the ice sheets surrounding continental Antartica are melting more rapidly than in recent years. Global warming over the next decade could possibly cause a rise in sea levels from a few feet, to a maximum of some 200 feet, in the unlikely event that all the ice in Antarctica was to melt".

Archie tried to picture the sea rising by this amount. It would certainly change the look of the seaside, he felt. The Brig continued, "This, in turn, taken with the effect of predicted levels of carbon dioxide released across the World today, would, in some scientists' opinions, not only make large areas of land uninhabitable but raise its temperature of the water to over the critical 2°C, which could then trigger an irreversible rise of temperature to the point where life on much of the planet would become unsustainable.

There is, worldwide, growing concern about Global Warming. Both Archie and Wallace looked dutifully worried, though Wallace felt better too hot than too cold and anyway, none of this seemed likely to happen in his lifetime. The Brig reminded them that this was a classic example of where States needed urgently to work together to re-assess the risk and agree what measures should now be taken to confront this extremely worrying threat.

Uncertainty and consequent risk is always around in this World, he felt. As you age, the odds anyway becoming increasingly stacked against you. When you cross the road, there is a risk. With care, you can minimize it, but you can't entirely remove it, as exemplified by statistics of traffic deaths. "You can't guard against devastating virus's or even, far less probably, being killed by an earthquake destroying your house, if you stay indoors, or being struck by lightning, if you don't. Risk assessment is an essential skill we all have to learn from childhood - sometimes the hard way.. How much should we adjust our way of life to seek to reduce these risks?

How real are they? Does the fact that some individuals and even some countries are cannot afford/obtain sufficient food, with resultant starvation and disease, whilst some individuals have greater personal assets than the entire wealth of some of those smaller countries, really matter? And, if so what can be done about it?" Neither he nor Archie knew the answer to such questions, though Wallace assumed the air of an expert in that field—money was something he had never had to worry about!.

The Brig pointed out that perceived and actual risks are often quite different. "For example," he said, "the risk of getting a rare disease can be far lower than that of being hit by a bus, but once one or more members of your family are so diagnosed, this risk is seen to be proportionally higher. For those actually hit by the proverbial bus, the reverse, of course, is true. Sometimes we can precisely quantify the risk. Usually, perhaps fortunately, we can't", he added. As science advances", he continued, "We will be able, more and more accurately, to make such assessments by analysis and manipulation of input data. And then we can, in theory anyway, see what actions are needed, if any, to minimize the risk".

Wallace thought to himself how boring life would, in that case, become. For Staffordshire Bull Terriers anyway, the risk of a scrap was the spice of life, but, of course, death and disease were something else, but why waste time on worrying about risks you can't do anything about? "If something happened to me", The Brig reminded him, "you would rapidly find a sharp drop in the quality of your life—with a move to kennels if you were lucky or the knackers yard if you were not". Wallace looked suitably contrite and planted an unexpected lick on an exposed knee. The Brig continued, with a smile, "even if I don't actually drop dead, your situation can suddenly deteriorate—things, for mutts like you, can quickly go unexpectedly wrong. The door to a room shuts; and you are on your own. If the house catches on fire and/or fills with smoke, you can only hope someone hears you and lets you out in time".

Wallace still remembered vividly when his luck had, seemingly run out. After a visit to the garden, covered in snow in midwinter, with the temperature well below zero, he found the garden door to the house had shut. His pitiful whimpers, seeking attention, went unheard for nearly two hours. Out there in the freezing cold, scratching at the firmly shut door, he probably was wondering whether he would survive the night, for his pampered lifestyle had left him rather soft and unprepared for such an eventuality. From his point of view, there was little he could do except wait patiently (or impatiently) at the door and make appropriate noises and scratches, hoping it would open. When it did, a couple of hours later, after The Brig had noted his absence, he showed no resentment and made no complaint; just a shiver, then a wriggle of joy and affection.

The Brig went on, "Dog owners can also easily be forgetful, careless, lazy or cruel. There are many who will, for one reason or another, let their 'pet' down and fail to meet that part of the bargain set out in the unwritten 'animal rights' constitution, where companionship, guard duties, unconditional love and acceptance of human rules are offered in exchange for accommodation, food, water and exercise. However, even if the will is there, things can easily go unexpectedly wrong. Perhaps I might have to go out for a couple of hours, leaving you, warm, fed and happy. Then, unexpectedly, I could be injured in a car accident and taken to hospital. A suitably located person would need to be told that you were in the house alone—otherwise you would just have to stay there, increasingly thirsty, hungry until, if you were lucky, someone came along, perhaps at the sound of your bark or whimper".

There were those too, The Brig reminded Wallace, who under sufficient financial pressure, would abandon their dog, as did Wilson's first owner. Some, too, would deliberately train them to fight, or use them as a status symbol to dominate their neighbours; and some will treat them throughout their lives with callous indifference or even outright brutality, regardless of the pain and suffering they cause. By this time, Wallace had become very quiet. Somewhere in his psychic memory was perhaps the long forgotten past of his ancestor's dog fights in the mining villages of Staffordshire.

Archie, who also had also been unusually silent, gave Wallace a comforting pat and then unexpectedly enquired, apropos their earlier debate, "Why did that reporter mention Virus's, Grandpa? Do you always catch diseases from others or are they sometimes something you just inherit?" The Brig acknowledged another of Archie's astute questions. He also gave Wallace a pat, before replying, "Particularly where there is shortage of food and water, diseases can rapidly spread and that sort of spread is what the reporter was referring to. However, diseases can just be passed on or inherited." There is nothing much a dog can do about that, Wallace thought. The Brig continued, picking up that concern. "For humans, though, a parent, for example, with Huntingdon's Disease (a rare neurodegenerative disease) now knows that he/she has a fifty-fifty chance of passing this disease on to their child, through the handing down of their defective gene.

However, prenatal checks of cells, or even 'artificial' impregnation (by inserting sperm into eggs already checked out to ensure they are not carrying the faulty gene) can remove this risk, should those concerned consider this technique to be affordable; and ethically and legally acceptable". Archie looked thoughtful. The Brig continued, "There is now, though, given early screening, the option of aborting a fetus, if the risks of it carrying a life threatening disease are considered high enough; enabling the parent to 'try again'. Hence, the term 'Designer Babies', coined by newspapers.

For, fertility regulations in the UK now allow doctors, with the consent of the potential parent, to destroy embryos affected by more than a hundred genetic conditions, including for illnesses that are not life threatening" Wallace, clearly bored by all this disease stuff, moved off to investigate another inviting smell. Archie was struggling too, but, fully immersed in a subject dear to his heart, The Brig kept going. "In many diseases", he went on, "there is some level of 'genetic susceptibility', even though the risk of the disease actually appearing is usually far, far lower than that for say 'Huntingdon's Disease'.

Both cancer and comparatively rare neurodegenerative diseases like 'Progressive Supranuclear Palsy' (from which, as described earlier Sara, the Brig's wife, had died), "involve a level of inherited genetic susceptibility, but an 'environmental trigger' is still required to set it off. In other words, in many diseases, such susceptibility is a necessary but not sufficient requirement for the disease to take hold. So, although it is now possible to screen for such genes and identify many of them, the risk of the environment providing this trigger cannot, even approximately, be quantified." Archie's eyes had begun to glaze over and Wallace moved off.

However, The Brig was not to be stopped. He continued, "Meanwhile, as scanning the human genome (revealing in ever more detail its genetic makeup) to find genetic variations associated with a particular disease has become easier and cheaper. This technology has also become an increasingly attractive means for police to track down criminal activity, insurance companies to assess risk and the State to fight terrorism. Some Governments may soon seek to legislate for the universal provision and data storage of DNA and related information.

This would enable them to monitor ever more closely their citizens' behavior and lives, leading, some fear, to '1984' scenarios and 'police states'. Insurance companies too are also now becoming much more interested in identifying genetic susceptibility of individuals, so that they can seek to reflect risk in the premiums they charge for life insurance, even though the links between susceptibility and development are still largely unknown."

Archie, who had been, for the last ten minutes, lying back on the grass, enjoying the sun (but still half listening), unexpectedly asked, "What are designer babies, Grandpa?" The Brig, realizing that he had obviously lost his audience some while back, checked, then replied, "Although the term 'designer babies' is still largely 'newspaper hype', science is moving fast and the manipulation of genes (and their coding letters) is more and more possible. By the time you get married, Archie, you will probably be able to choose some of the characteristics of your baby, including sex and the colour of its hair— blond or brunette, boy or girl?—your choice, although undoubtedly it will cost you", he added.

Archie sat up sharply, perhaps working out his preferences. Wallace, who had returned from marking a particularly interesting piece of grass, was, again, on his back, looking at the colour of his hair, with some apparent satisfaction. The Brig concluded, he felt sagely, "As you grow up, there will always be uncertainty; and more and more difficult choices to be made, based on perceived risk and reward". Neither Archie nor Wallace appeared, the Brig felt, particularly impressed by this, in his view, important piece of wisdom. It was time to move off. They gathered themselves up, collected Archie's suitcase and moved off to the car, deep in thought. Wallace was clearly sad to see Archie leave.

# Chapter 8

## *Ageing and illness*

AS HE GREW OLDER, WALLACE began perceptibility to slow down. He still enjoyed his morning walks and routine games, but sometimes on an afternoon walk, he would, especially in the cold, go on strike, refusing to move on and shivering, with a pitiful look. "Don't make me go any further, Dad".

The vet diagnosed arthritis and suggested Glucosamine and Chondroitin pills or sardines, which help maintain healthy joints, might help. The Brig found, however, that getting him to swallow the former was not so easy. However, by pushing a pill each morning into a third of a sausage, Wallace could be tricked into swallowing both.

Taking these daily, Wallace was off again, at the start of the day, as of old, full of life and energy. However, in the afternoon, there were longer periods now during which he just took himself off to doze, lying full length, preferably in the sun, with his head between his paws. After an hour or two, whilst The Brig was at his desk, he would bustle into the study, full of energy again. Given any encouragement, he would then, like a jack-in-the-box lap dog, leap onto 'Dad's' knees and seek to make a quick lick.

**Wallace leaves work**

An invitation such as *"Where is your ball—seek it out"*, would always set him off to search around the house for an object that could represent a ball and encourage anyone around to chase him and take it from him, tossing it in the air to tempt them to grab it. He was amazingly skillful in keeping it just out of reach, until both parties were exhausted. Then he would stretch out and lie peacefully at The Brig's feet, occasionally grunting quietly with pleasure and lazily wagging his tail.

However, walking in the garden that November, the Brig first noticed Wallace was finding it difficult to keep his balance, when he lifted his leg. He had always had this astonishingly exaggerated lift when making his mark as opposed to a much more delicate lift to relieve himself. Like many other male dogs, he has an equally astonishing ability to keep enough reserve in the tank to continue to make as many marks as needed, when and where he deemed necessary, during even the longest walk, and would still be marking away happily some two hours later.

Marking was often followed by a demonstration of strength, with some sharp pawing of the ground with both front and rear legs. Now, however, he began to fall over when lifting his leg and have increasing difficulty in descending the stairs. It was also noticeable that his jaw and cheek on the right hand side (facing front) was drooping and the reflex in his right eye was almost nonexistent. Very worried, The Brig took him to the vet in Towcester.

She carried out several tests, though was particularly concerned about his right eye. She feared he might well have a brain tumor, though there were, she recognized, other less frightening possibilities. If it were to be a tumor, the sooner it was detected the better, for his chance of survival. Wallace needed to be taken urgently to a specialist, for an MRI scan and lumber puncture, to confirm her tentative diagnosis.

Fortunately, The Brig had a Pet Insurance Plan, as the specialist bill was likely to be eye wateringly high. There was a top Animal Medical Centre just off the MI near London, with veterinary surgeons and all the high tech equipment and scanners of a hospital, so he booked Wallace in there and drove him down the next Monday, having meanwhile said a quiet prayer for a successful outcome. The Centre was very modern and impressive. They were met that morning around 9am by a young receptionist and, after a short wait, taken to a charming French Surgeon, with a string of initials after his name and warm and a friendly manner. He quickly made friends with Wallace and looked him over, noting his lack of reflexes and problem with balance. He said that he needed an MRI scan, a lumbar puncture and blood tests to help make a diagnosis. He added quietly, "We should not be too optimistic". The examination would take all day.

He asked The Brig to sign up to agree a diagnostic plan involving scanning and blood tests for Wallace and sought agreement to 'put him down', if a serious brain tumor was present, then said, "We will be careful. Please ring after 4pm to confirm a time and then come back to collect him". After giving Wallace a loving hug, The Brig reluctantly left him with the Frenchman. He then drove off a few miles and down a track to a field with, in the morning sunshine, a beautiful view on top of the downs, to contemplate. It was a stunningly lovely day.

Struggling to come to terms with the diagnosis, The Brig feared the worst and the dreaded decision to be made should Wallace have an incurable cancer. For, if it had advanced as in Wilson's case, it would be the kindest thing—a last loving gift—for him to be given a lethal injection. Shaking his head and reminding himself to 'get a grip', he drove rather miserably on to his Sister's house, fortunately only a few miles away.

She too was an arch animal lover and her house was, accordingly, full of cats and dogs, with chickens and horses outside. The two of them philosophized on life and dogs over lunch and after a walk in the beautiful Hertfordshire countryside near Stevenage (accompanied by the aforementioned dogs), they enjoyed together a family update and an afternoon cup of tea. It was then time to telephone the Veterinary Centre—a call The Brig dreaded. A Receptionist answered the call. She did not know how things had gone and just said she had been asked to request that The Brig be at the Clinic by 6pm. As he approached it just before the due time, he prepared for and rehearsed acceptance of the worst, before walking in to hear the verdict. Accordingly, he went straight up to the Receptionist to ask how Wallace was.

Straight faced and stern, she just said "Please take a seat". So he waited. Twenty long minutes later, a nurse appeared pushing Wallace into Reception on a trolley, on which he lay at full stretch, looking very miserable, whimpering quietly and covered with bandages. The Brig followed her and Wallace to the door to the French Vet's Office and apprehensively entered. After an eternal few seconds, the Frenchman broke into a broad smile and said, "I am happy to inform you that Wallace does not have cancer". As his words sank in, the Brig was sorely tempted to give him a Gallic hug. However, resisting this temptation, he asked quietly, "So, what is your diagnosis, then?"

Perhaps sensing the rejected intent, the Frenchman hurriedly but politely offered him a seat and then continued, "Until we have finished our tests, we will not be sure what is wrong, but I strongly suspect a deep ear infection. Here are some antibiotics", he said, passing over a large packet, "Wallace needs to take three of these tablets a day for the next four weeks. I will ring you when the test results are available". Looking at the trolley in which Wallace lay, he added, "Wallace will be fully recovered from the anesthetic in about thirty minutes. In all probability, he will be OK to walk to the car. Meanwhile, if you have any questions, I would be pleased to try and answer them." The Brig just felt great relief and joy. He asked if the condition was in any way life threatening. "Definitely not", said the Frenchman, with a smile. He would, of course, inform Helen Pope (Wallace's vet in Towcester), of his diagnosis in the next 24 hours, but was confident of a complete recovery.

The Brig thanked him and the two shook hands. Half an hour later, the nurse helped lift Wallace out of the trolley and, accompanied by the Frenchman, he wobbled to the exit. Once gently lifted into the car, Wallace gave The Brig a lick and settled, with a long sigh, into a tight ball, then slept quietly, high on pain killers, on the journey home. With his thrice daily antibiotics, he started to slowly recover, but, after a few weeks, once again, worryingly unwell.

Once more, The Brig took him back to the Towcester Vet for advice. She suggested a small operation, which involved shortening the length of the lip on that side of his face to pull it in, as an infection was beginning to spread to his teeth. The following day, they went through the 'please take a seat' routine and paperwork signing, before Wallace was, once again, taken off for his anesthetic and operation. Returning that evening, The Brig was, again, enormously relieved to see him still alive and well but very wobbly and forlorn, with a wriggly tail wag and lopsided grin. The Receptionist provided some more antibiotics and pain killers for him to be given three times a day. Staffordshire Bull Terries are renowned for their stoicism, but his lip was obviously really hurting, as he lay in his basket, quietly moaning, on his return home that night. To everyone's delight, however, he steadily improved over the next week and soon began to feel his old self again. The infection was gone, though his mouth had become endearingly slightly shortened on the right side, with one tooth showing.

Some two years went by. Wallace was now outwardly fully recovered but now only enjoyed shorter walks (which took longer, with more time spent sniffing out territory). He increasingly sought, too, to double back when less than halfway along one of their established routes and would give a pleading look, asking to return to the garden gate then across the grass back home. He was also panting more noticeably and drinking more, stopping off at any pond for a quick refill. It was again time to take him in for his annual check up. The Vet was concerned about the amount of water he was drinking and his heavy panting. After a close inspection, during which Wallace made clear that he was not enjoying the experience, she diagnosed possible Cushing's disease.

This was, she said, effectively a liver disorder but, although life threatening, treatable. A blood sample was required to confirm the tentative finding. This was taken the following week but proved inconclusive, so The Brig and Wallace had to return for further tests, involving specifically three more blood samples to be taken at one hour intervals. Meanwhile, there were still some good shorter walks around Towcester. The two set off, after the first sample, for what turned out to be a very enjoyable shorter walk through the nearby fields, along a 'right of way' track, before returning in time for the second sample. As they were, by then, both 'walked out', they returned by car to Wappenham for coffee for the former and biscuits for the latter, before returning for a third visit.

Two days later they drove, once again, to the Veterinary Centre to hear the results. Wallace apparently, after all, did not have Cushing's Disease but a serious liver disorder, or more probably, Helen Pope feared, cancer of the liver. In either case, there was no treatment other than a major operation, which would, she felt, only be helpful, if the cancer had not already spread. At his age, she did not recommend this route anyway, though she said, when pressed, that it would be possible to carry out an ultra-scan and then if necessary a biopsy to obtain a liver sample. This would allow a definite diagnosis, but at Wallace's age a major operation to remove part of the liver was not something she would recommend.

Her gentle advice was to accept that he probably had only some nine months pain free life left. The two left in silence, former paying yet another sizeable bill and the latter just happy to leave the centre.

The Brig would telephone her later about symptoms and palliative care. All dog owners are painfully aware of the mismatch between man and dog in the ageing process; and the inevitability of that day when they must face saying goodbye to the friend they love. There was nothing either of them could do about it other than just 'kick on' and enjoy together the time left to them. This was very much in line with Wallace's philosophy—enjoy the present and let the future take care of itself!

However, the ultra-scan was inconclusive and Helen Pope agreed that a biopsy using a mini camera to guide a small cutting tool through a small opening to be made in Wallace's stomach to obtain a liver sample was perhaps, after all, a worthwhile option. For this would provide the essential data for a decision to be taken to see what more, if anything, could be done. She carried out the operation the next day. The Brig dropped Wallace off in the morning and anxiously awaited the outcome. They would ring after the operation. He was to return to collect him if all went well. The welcome call came late morning. Wallace was recovering from the anesthetic after a successful operation and could be collected that afternoon. He was very unsteady and sore, but, with his painkillers, he was ready to come home and curl up in his basket in the study. For the next two days, whilst The Brig again anxiously awaited the results of the biopsy and liver sample examination, Wallace was pretty miserable but by day three was back on his feet and able to take short little walks.

On the third day, Helen Pope called. The news was good. He did not have cancer. He did not have Cushing's Disease. He had some liver disorder, which was not, after all, life threatening. Wallace was now approaching thirteen and life expectancy for a Staffie of his age was not more than a year or two at most. The Brig, however, was happy that it was likely that the two of them still had at least that time together and preferred not to look further ahead to the date, when Wallace, or he (dependent on who eventually went first!), might learn at last 'The meaning of life'. That was, as the Brig later noted, nearly a year ago, and they were both still in fairly good order. In fact, Wallace was now managing nine holes at Farthingstone Golf Course again, with a new lease of life.

# Chapter 9

## *The Meaning of life*

WALLACE, IN ANIMAL TERMS, WAS by now some ten years older that The Brig, using the normal seven year dog to man multiplier. He was already 'of a good age'; and taking the average Staffordshire Bull Terrier's life expectancy—though he would never accept being described as average—doing pretty well. He had maybe some seven times one more year or some seven dog years left to enjoy, hopefully, a pain free life. Anything might happen over that time He was, like The Brig, growing noticeably older, but perhaps more gracefully and graciously. His muzzle was greying, and, despite his daily Chondroitin and Glucosamine pills, he stiffened up after walks, clearly still suffering a bit from arthritis.

His grin was more lopsided than ever and he spent more time asleep or stretched out zen-like by the fire. They had both definitely slowed down and were becoming used to living with the small but growing irritations of age. One or other of them, The Brig assumed, would die first in the not too distant future. It was still not quite clear which of them it would go first, he felt, though, the odds were increasingly pointing toward Wallace, as The Brig remained stubbornly fit. If it were, after all, however, The Brig, who would then look after him? Would anyone or would Wallace just have to be put down? The Brig was confident that one of his long suffering sons would take Wallace on, if only to prevent them being haunted!

Many would say, though, he was only a dog and that he had already had more than his fair share of life's good fortune—thoroughly spoilt and pampered over the last ten years, with his meat from the Towcester butcher's shop grilled to taste and good friends coming in to look after him at home and walk him when The Brig was away. They might well be right! They might too be unenthusiastic about taking on an old Staffordshire Bull-Terrier, maybe through fear of the reputation of this breed and reports of their somewhat aggressive attitude to other male dogs. Wallace had only been in a kennel once in his life and would absolutely hate to be put in one now, but it could be difficult both for him and any new 'owner' to settle into a productive relationship in a loving home at his age, with such a limited expectancy of life.

Of course, like everyone else, he would just have to adapt and 'kick on' until it was time for him to 'move on' too. For The Brig, Wallace had always been a patient, undemanding, demonstratively loving and much loved companion, without whom life for him would have been immensely poorer. Would they meet again after they both had departed this world, he sometime, in a maudlin way, wondered. Are dogs allowed in heaven, if heaven really exists?

Heaven would be, for The Brig—should he make it there—a lesser place without him. Wallace had exhibited such wonderful qualities of love, loyalty, patience and courage and, of course, was an essential participator in their philosophical debates. It would be so very final, if death meant 'never no more'. Should Wallace die first, as now seemed likely, The Brig would see those loving eyes, feel the soft sheen of his oyster ears, hear his grunts and imagine his wriggly greetings for the rest of his life.

His wife, Sara's death in 1995 had forced him to face and come to terms with what the loss of someone really close meant. The curious and comforting thing for him, was that she remained, in a different dimension (perhaps one of those seven extra dimensions predicted in the Superstring Theory) definitely around much of the time, in one form or another. When, too often, The Brig strayed from the straight and narrow guidance of his conscience and followed his own selfish designs, she was not slow to chide. This made him hopeful, if not certain that, anyway for us humans, there is a promise of life after death. His faith was not quite strong enough, he had to admit, to be sure, though that part of him, brought up in the Anglican Church, still strongly believed anyway in the broader truth of what it teaches—most of the time!

However, he continued to worry about what happens to animals after their death; and particularly what had happened to Wilson and what would happen to Wallace. The latter had been his constant and loyal companion for the previous thirteen years now. He has found a special place in the later life of The Brig, who would miss him terribly. He would for the rest of his life, continue to hope and believe that they would all meet again. And if and when it came to judgement time, he would speak out for Wallace and his unconditional love for his family and hope that God would treat him kindly.

The Brig reflected, looking at Wallace curled up on the floor by his feet, that whatever our short-term or long-term goals, all of us must look forward (well, in another sense, not look forward) to our appointed time and manner of departure. How will we each cope, he thought, when the moment arrives? Faith in some future existence—perhaps another go in this World or maybe a more perfect world somewhere else—can clearly give people great strength and fortitude in facing their eventual inevitable departure from this life.

For some of us, he reflected, death will come unexpectedly and quickly. For others, there will be perhaps a premonition or indication and possibly fear and pain en route. For many, it will come from an incurable disease, where its approach can be measured in terms of medically assessed life expectancy. What is certain though is that we—dogs and humans alike—will all have to face this moment of dying in one way or another, one day. In moments of reflection, we recognize this as a necessary event—just imagine for a minute the appalling alternative of living for ever—even though we don't exactly look forward to dying.

On 12th June 2005, Steve Jobs, then CEO of Apple Computers and of Pixar Animation Studios, summed death up brilliantly in an impressive address delivered to students at an American University.

*"No one wants to die. Even people who want to go to heaven don't want to die to get there. And yet death is the destination we all share. No one has ever escaped it. And that is as it should be, because death is very likely the single best invention of life. It is life's change agent. It clears out the old to make way for the new. Right now the new is you, but someday not too long from now, you will gradually become the old and be cleared away".*

# Chapter 10

## *Some Tentative Conclusions*

IF WALLACE DIED FIRST, THE Brig knew he would miss him dreadfully. His wriggle of joy, his grunt of happiness, his grin, his companionship, his warmth, his loveable eccentricities and the unashamed love he has given him, would remain with The Brig the rest of his life, but—whatever the future might hold—life would still go on. For those of us who believe, death is anyway no more than another stage in our journey and God will always give those leaving this world the strength to bear the pain and suffering of departure. Nevertheless, even for these lucky ones, it must be a frightening moment as death approaches. Just imagine, for a moment, placing your head on a block, with the executioner standing there with his axe poised. You stretch out your arms for the coup de grace. You may be on route to heaven but it must be a route you would prefer to postpone.

For others, it is doubly frightening. Firstly, there remains the fear that this might be the absolute end, then nothing for eternity, except perhaps if fortunate, for our genes to be passed on. And for those without a child of their own, their genes are likely to wither away. Secondly, we all can imagine a least favourite and most painful way of departing this world and hope and/or pray that such a worst case scenario does not come our way. For this second concern, there remains, for dogs, a loving owner to help them at the last and for humans an escape route for those who have the means, the capability, the time and the strength of will to 'put themselves' down. In most countries, suicide is not against and is anyway effectively beyond the law. You clearly cannot punish someone for killing themselves.

Moving on from the controversial area of helping someone else to die, discussed earlier, The Brig reflected, that everyone, sooner or later, asks themselves questions like, "When I die, what happens?" and, "Why am I here?" Logic can't answer these simple questions. If it could, then there would be no need for faith. For those without faith, the questions might then be, "What is the point?" and "If we are all here by chance, what then is our purpose in life? To increase our species, as some Darwinists believe?"

The Bible and faiths around the world seek to give guidance on life's meaning and purpose, but the faith required to accept what they offer, means—in some cases—the overturning of the laws of physics and logic. The wonderful life and even the death of Christ and its dreadful but awe inspiring manner can be proved to be factual, but his resurrection and ascension to heaven flies in the face of science and logic; yet belief that this actually happened is an essential element of the Christian faith. However, the majority of the world's population are not Christians and there are many non-believers. Is their alternative or non-belief therefore wrong? Could that condemn them to eternal nothingness, when they die? And how do we reconcile a God who cares for the human race and loves each and every one of us, with the terrible things that happen to people and animals?

He (or perhaps She) seems, at times, uninterested or perhaps worse impotent in face of natural and 'man made' disasters. Is man so important anyway? Are other alien species across the universe doing better and does God give them equal or greater love? What about all those other species on this planet? Does God love them too and does he judge them by their performance on earth? Impossible questions to answer other than by faith. There appears to be no overwhelming logic behind the argument that we are especially chosen. In the scale of the universe, we, the human race, are, in many respects, irrelevant in the same sense that a particle within an element of an atom is irrelevant to us. We have to recognize that there could be millions of other life forms on millions of other planets

Yet, many of us feel strongly that there is something within us, telling us there is a clear purpose in each of our lives. It is up to us to try and fulfil this purpose as best we can, guided by our conscience. We all feel, to some degree, a sense of right and wrong. Some wrongs are clear cut. Some acts are clearly despicable. Others are conflicting and blurred, as are our choices and actions. Yet everyone desperately needs some compass to steer by. If there were no God, there would be no firm basis of moral behavior or for agonizing discussion and decisions about right and wrong. The moral maze would be entirely subjective, if resolved solely by imposed man made laws of the land. And on what would these be based? Fairness, equality and love your neighbor are surely deeper seated motives than just evolved through social needs. And why do things you have done 'wrong' in your life bother you so much as you grow older? On what basis were they wrong?

Our conscience will, if we listen, give us guidance through many of the perplexities and difficulties of life. But what is conscience and how does it work. Is it just a social phenomenon? Many religions argue that on this planet, only mankind has a conscience and a soul; and that we alone of all the living species are made in God's image. To some, this smacks of arrogance, for surely, if there is a designer, all species have been designed by that designer, with some purpose? And, in order to follow that purpose, they too need a compass.

We all—humans and animals alike—strut and fret our hour upon the stage of life in this world, many of us without a clear idea of why we are here or what we are expected to achieve. Without direction from above, we muddle through the moral maze, steered, perhaps some if not all the time by our conscience—that elusive compass—which points, for Christians, toward what is set out in The Bible; or perhaps just toward the laws of the land in which we live. Money, fame or 'success in life' (how is this judged?) are all doubtful goals in the end analysis, though hard not to seek at the time.

The Brig's conscience was always there nagging him with suggestions and answers. "Do as you would be done by", it often reminded him. He knew what he should do, but the Devil was devilishly skilful at arguing why he should do something else. And how is this conscience driven? Do dogs know what is right and wrong? Sometimes they seem to! Life is a puzzlement, as the King said to Anna in 'The King and I'. On a personal note, The Brig found Wallace may not have had much of a conscience, as we know it, but unlike many humans, always forgave and offered his 'Dad' total loyalty and unconditional love, whatever the provocation. If he is not made in God's image, then neither am I, thought The Brig.

He fully recognized that he had been extremely lucky throughout his life. With four sons, thirteen grandchildren and many relations and friends, he would, with or without Wallace, always have had those whom he loved, in his mind. He sometimes felt that to have no one to love, or worse, to be the only living creature inhabiting the world or even the universe would truly be hell.

In the beginning of time, perhaps God faced that appalling status? Could that be his reason for starting the universe? To have someone to love? But unless a living creature has freedom of choice, can he or she be described as living?

This must be God's conundrum. Offer freedom and 'wrong' choices will be made (Adam and Eve). Don't offer freedom and you have no true companion. Over the history of the universe, the results to date sometimes seemed to The Brig to reflect poorly on God's choice of humans as those to love; and, on this earth as the master species.

Maybe, after all, elsewhere across the Universe we are not; or maybe we are, but are unlikely remain long as such. It has to be said, at the end, that Wallace, whom this book is all about, never, in any of these philosophical debates with his 'Dad', showed any real interest in 'all that stuff', as he would describe the above. Life, in his view has always been about today, and let yesterday and tomorrow take care of themselves. What will be, will be. And yet—Wallace had taught him much, over some thirteen years, most of all about loyalty and that unconditional love we all need to take us through the knocks of life and finally through to our departure from this World.

# Postscript

BY 2012, WALLACE WAS GETTING noticeably older. He was spending more time lying in the sun and either sleeping or watching what was going around him and less and less on active walks. On one such walk at Farthingstone golf course (where he had some while earlier been accepted as a 'dog' member, in the same way as had his predecessor, Wilson) he had struggled up the steep hill on the first hole and then collapsed on reaching the edge of the green.

It was a beautiful sunny day. He just gently laid down by the Green and looked up at The Brig. "I can't walk any further, Dad", he seemed to say. Anyway. He just couldn't get up. The Brig didn't think he could carry him all the way back (Wallace was quite a heavy dog by then), so he had to run back himself to get special permission to drive his car up along the edge of the fairway, pick Wallace up and, with him on board, drive back to the Club House.

After giving Wallace a drink of water, The Brig explained the problem to The Club Secretary, who he knew well. The latter then kindly offered to look after Wallace, whilst The Brig and his friends returned to their planned 9 holes. The Brig was seriously worried, but all agreed that Wallace would definately want them to carry on. So it was agreed that he would remain at the Club House and, as a privileged dog, be looked after by the Club Secretary!

On finishing his nine holes of golf (which, unsurprisingly hadn't gone that well), The Brig hurried back to the Clubhouse to see how Wallace was. Thankfully, he was looking almost his old self and wagged his tail furiously when he spotted The Brig. So, after thanking The Club Secretary, they returned home together. All seemed well. However, a few days later, when The Brig took him on a short walk in Bucknell Woods, Wallace just collapsed again and The Brig had to carry him back to the car.

Then, on the day before the Annual PSP Association Charity Golf Competition, The Brig drove with Wallace into Towcester and parked in the Waitrose Car Park to purchase some food supplies, including a small meaty bone for a small treat for Wallace to make up a bit for leaving him behind the next day. It was a beautiful autumn day. During their short walk outside Waitrose, The Brig offered him this bone, which he attempted to swallow in one gulp. It stuck in his throat. He immediately made huge efforts to 'cough it up', but without success. Seriously alarmed, The Brig helped him back to the car and drove straight to the nearby veterinary centre.

After the usual wait, Wallace was examined and the vets advised that the best course was to take him home and allow him time to successfully swallow it. The pair of them returned home, anxiously. They had several walks in the garden without success. That night, The Brig put a sleeping bag down on the floor downstairs and lay close to Wallace, who was clearly still in pain. They went out into the garden at regular intervals through the night, with Wallace attempting to cough the bone up or swallow it, but without success. Neither of them slept much, if at all. The veterinary centre opened at 7.30 am. The Brig drove Wallace straight there then. The Vet, when the Brig explained that he had to drive to near Woking that morning (to run the Annual PSPA Golf Competition there), suggested they take Wallace in for the day. The Brig reluctantly agreed and, giving Wallace a quick hug, promising to be back that evening

He then drove off to Woking and the Golf competition, arriving at the course just in time and set off almost immediately with his team around the eighteen holes. Unsurprisingly, he found it difficult to concentrate and played rather badly. After the last four had completed their round and scores had been added up and checked, they held their prize giving ceremony, with The Brig giving his usual thankyou speech on behalf of PSPA and then he anxiously departed for home.

Despite the slow progress around London on the M25, The Brig was back in Towcester just after 7pm. However, the veterinary centre had however already closed for the night and on his return home, there was no answer to his telephone call to ask them about how Wallace was. The Brig rang early the next morning to be gently informed that Wallace had been in increasing pain during the night and, as there was nothing they could do to help. They had tried to contact The Brig that evening (whilst he was driving back from Woking) but without success. That night as Wallace's pain level rose, they had been forced to give him a lethal injection, being the kindest thing for him. He had died peacefully, shortly after midnight.

Early the next morning, The Brig drove straight to the veterinary centre and spent a few minutes alone with Wallace, whose body had been carried to a quiet room. He gave him one last hug and told him how much he loved him. He then said a sad goodbye, ruffled his back and then walked slowly back to his car. If there is/was a dog's heaven, The Brig was sure he would be there, despite his occasional misdemeanors.

Perhaps, thought The Brig, we might even meet again there or in another life. After Sara's death, he had been The Brig's closest companion for twelve years, and one of the best of friends. They had seen more of each other than any other living creature over this time, though The Brig's four sons and their families were and remain, as he ages, his pride and joy. His regular visits to them and their four families keep him in close touch with them all, as well as his probably irritatingly regular telephone and Skype calls. Everyone told The Brig, after Wallace's death, that he should 'get another dog' but he just couldn't. He still hopes/dreams that perhaps one day, in another life, he will meet up with Wallace again and perhaps even 'discuss more scientific concerns and 'get to the bottom of things' as they once did.

He also really wanted to explain to Wallace why he had just left him with the Vet that day, when he was dying, and needed The Brig's company. "It's always upset me that I wasn't with him in the end" he told his family "I'd like Wallace to know just how much I loved him and would never have left him that day if I'd known what he was facing". Whatever his faults, Wallace had, in The Brig's view anyway, earned his place in dogs' heaven alongside Wilson. "I will always miss him very much", The Brig confessed. "Though, he added, with a small smile, not as much as Sara".

# Brigadier Michael R Koe Obe

EDUCATED AT SANDROYD SCHOOL, MARLBOROUGH College and The Royal Military Academy Sandhurst, Michael was sent, as a young intelligence officer, to Washington DC during the Kennedy era, after which he served with the Royal Green Jackets in Penang, Borneo, Berlin, Cyprus, Tidworch, and Northern Ireland. His final posting was to Rheindahlen, as Brigadier General Staff Intelligence of the British Army of the Rhine and Northern Army Group. He attended e Royal Military College of Science (BSc Engr), Staff College (psc) and the Joint Services Staff College (jssc). He left the Army in 1984 to join a Defence and Security Company in Jordan and London. He and his wife Sara moved up to Northamptonshire in 1987. In 1992, Sara was diagnosed as having a comparatively rare neurodegenerative disease, Progressive Supranuclear Palsy (PSP). Details of this devastating disease and of the charity itself, which they set up together in 1994, can be found at www.pspeur.org. is was the subject of his first book, 'Charity Begins at Home' published in 2007. Sara died from PSP in January 1994. He continued to run the Charity until 2011. He has four sons, all married, and thirteen grandchildren.

Lightning Source UK Ltd.
Milton Keynes UK
UKHW020259080223
416610UK00016B/2028